Members of the Jewish resistance are captured by SS troops (*Schutzstaffel*, Hitler's powerful paramilitary organization) during the Warsaw ghetto uprising April 19–May 16, 1943. The original German caption reads: "These bandits offered armed resistance." The man on the left has raised his fist, an anti-fascist symbol of solidarity and defiance dating back to 1917.

WE MUST NOT FORGET

HOLOCAUST STORIES *of*
SURVIVAL *and* RESISTANCE

Indonesian Dutch rescuers with the Jewish child they are hiding in the Netherlands. Among those pictured are Alfred Münzer (right), Tolé Madna (center, holding Alfred), and Mima Saïna (far left). Although Alfred stood out as a Caucasian child, neither he nor the Madna family were denounced or turned in by neighbors.

Also by
Deborah Hopkinson

*We Had to Be Brave: Escaping the Nazis
on the Kindertransport*

D-Day: The World War II Invasion That Changed History

*Dive! World War II Stories of
Sailors & Submarines in the Pacific*

*Courage & Defiance: Stories of Spies, Saboteurs,
and Survivors in World War II Denmark*

Titanic: Voices from the Disaster

Up Before Daybreak: Cotton and People in America

*Shutting Out the Sky: Life in the Tenements
of New York, 1880–1924*

Jewish children who had been in hiding pose outside with Dutch children after the liberation of the Netherlands in April 1945.

WE MUST NOT FORGET

HOLOCAUST STORIES *of* SURVIVAL *and* RESISTANCE

Deborah Hopkinson

SCHOLASTIC
F●CUS

NEW YORK

All rights reserved. Published by Scholastic Focus, an imprint of
Scholastic Inc., *Publishers since 1920.* SCHOLASTIC, SCHOLASTIC FOCUS, and associated
logos are trademarks and/or registered trademarks of Scholastic Inc.

Library of Congress Cataloging-in-Publication Data

Names: Hopkinson, Deborah, author.
Title: We must not forget : Holocaust stories of survival and resistance /
Deborah Hopkinson.
Description: New York : Scholastic Focus, [2021] | Includes bibliographical references
and index. | Audience: Ages 8-12 | Audience: Grades 4-6 | Summary: "As World War II
raged, millions of young Jewish people were caught up in the horrors of the Nazis' Final
Solution. Many readers know of Adolf Hitler and the Nazi state's genocidal campaign
against European Jews and others of so-called "inferior" races. Yet so many of the
individual stories remain buried in time. Of those who endured the Holocaust, some
were caught by the Nazis and sent to concentration camps, some hid right under Hitler's
nose, some were separated from their parents, some chose to fight back. Against all
odds, some survived. They all have stories that must be told. They all have stories we
must keep safe in our collective memory. In this thoroughly researched and passionately
written narrative nonfiction for upper middle-grade readers, critically acclaimed author
Deborah Hopkinson allows the voices of Holocaust survivors to live on the page, recalling
their persecution, survival, and resistance. Focusing on testimonies across Germany, the
Netherlands, France, and Poland, Hopkinson paints a moving and diverse portrait of the
Jewish youth experience in Europe under the shadow of the Third Reich. With archival
images and myriad interviews, this compelling and beautifully told addition to Holocaust
history not only honors the courage of the victims, but calls young readers to action—
by reminding them that heroism begins with the ordinary, everyday feat of showing
compassion toward our fellow citizens"—Provided by publisher.
Identifiers: LCCN 2020014131 | ISBN 9781338255775 (hardcover) |
ISBN 9781338255782 (ebook)
Subjects: LCSH: Holocaust, Jewish (1939-1945)—Personal narratives—Juvenile literature.
| World War, 1939-1945—Personal narratives—Juvenile literature. | Jewish children in
the Holocaust—Biography—Juvenile literature. | Jewish youth—Europe—History—20th
century—Juvenile literature. | Europe—History—20th century—Biography.
Classification: LCC D804.34 .H676 2021 | DDC 940.53/18092535—dc23
LC record available at https://lccn.loc.gov/2020014131

1 2020

Printed in the U.S.A.   23
First edition, February 2021

Book design by Becky Terhune

For
Steven, Alex, Sylvie,
and Oliver,
with gratitude and love

When a country is overcome by hatred and fear, when war and massacres spread like the plague, there are nevertheless always a few men and women who do not join the pack. Without a word, they step aside. In secrecy and in danger, they prefer to help rather than denounce, protect rather than destroy.

—JACQUES SEMELIN

Adolf Hitler walks to his car after addressing an SA (abbreviation for *Sturmabteilung*, Hitler's assault division, also known as storm troopers or brownshirts) rally in the Berlin Lustgarten, a park in central Berlin. The rally in February of 1936 celebrated the third anniversary of his chancellorship.

THE LIGHT ANSWERS

A Hanukkah menorah rests on the sill of an apartment window in Kiel, Germany, in 1932.

The menorah belonged to Akiva Posner, the rabbi of Kiel. The family escaped. The menorah survived and is still in use. Rachel Posner, his wife, wrote on the back in German (rough translation here), with Judah referring to the kingdom of Judah, or Jews: "Death to Judah" the flag says—"Judah will live forever!" the light answers.

Hitler Youth on parade on May 1, 1933. A group of girls stands at attention with Nazi flags in the upper center of the photograph. The Hitler Youth organization began in 1926 and by 1938 had more than seven million members.

BERLIN, 1933

And now I see the "Führer"; his arm is raised and he's swinging it around as though in a trance. Deafening roar: *Sieg Heil!* [Hail Victory!] *Heil Hitler!*

The crowd is closing in. A voice shouts, "Hey you, where's your arm?"

Another voice: "I saw that too! And her mouth is frozen shut."

"Hey, is something wrong with you?"

How can I be so stupid? What *is* wrong with me? Never occurred to me that everyone here would be a follower . . . How am I going to get out of here? I'm so wedged in I can't even move. The first man who started harassing me is yelling, "Where's the arm?"

. . . But raising my arm now won't help, and anyway . . . no.

. . . And we thought we were prepared. We have a lot to learn, even that there may be a time when we have to raise an arm to save ourselves. There will be great sacrifices. But we can't be afraid now; fear is crippling, and we must make our voices heard.

After all, this can't last for long.

—Lisa Eckstein Fittko, *a Jewish anti-fascist activist who fled Germany in 1933. From then until 1941, she and her husband, Hans Fittko, helped Jews, writers, and others escape into Spain. The couple immigrated to Chicago in 1948. In recognition of her work, the Federal Republic of Germany awarded her the Distinguished Service Medal, First Class, in 1986. Lisa died in 2005 at age ninety-five.*

TO GIVE THE DEAD A VOICE . . .

A young Jewish woman in the Lodz ghetto in Poland writes her last letter before being deported to Chelmno death camp in 1942.

When you have worked, as I have, for about fifteen years with these documents, you are continuously confronted with the dead, the voices of the deceased. I read these papers, the little scraps of paper, thrown from the train, the rare messages coming from Westerbork [internment and transit camp in the Netherlands] . . . Before me, hardly anyone has read them and, after me, they are locked into the archives and it's possible that nobody else will see them.

They awoke in me the awareness that one of the tasks of the historian, the man who writes about people of the past, is to give the dead a voice. The dead must be able to speak . . . and anyone who lets the dead remain silent allows them to die twice, and I have simply refused to permit that.

—**JACOB PRESSER,** *Danish historian and Holocaust survivor*

Dear Reader,

The heartbreaking story of Anne Frank and her sister, Margot, who hid with their parents in the Netherlands before being captured by the Nazis, has touched millions of readers. Yet there are so many more stories we need to know.

In this book, you'll meet Chella and Flora Velt, who, like the Frank sisters, were captured but, against all odds, survived. You'll read about a pair of young brothers who fled the Nazis across France; two teens who fell in love in a concentration camp; and a young woman, only seventeen when Germany invaded her home of Warsaw, Poland, who helped lead an uprising and spent the rest of her life dedicated to Holocaust education.

You'll also read about Ruth Oppenheimer David. I began to correspond with Ruth David, who turned ninety in 2019, while I was writing *We Had to Be Brave: Escaping the Nazis on the Kindertransport* (2020). When Ruth was ten, her parents sent her from Germany to safety in England. When World War II was declared on September 3, 1939, the door to immigration slammed shut for Ruth's parents and two younger siblings, Michael (now Michel) and Feo. Michel and Feo traveled from France to England for Ruth's milestone birthday in 2019. How had they survived? I wanted to find out more about families like the Oppenheimers who were caught in Nazi-occupied Europe.

We Must Not Forget is not a comprehensive history of the Holocaust. The first section includes accounts from Germany and the Netherlands; the second focuses on France; the third on Poland. Each part opens with brief bios and key dates, so you don't have to go to the back to find that information. I do hope you'll explore the back section, though. It includes links to online resources such as the United States Holocaust Memorial Museum (USHMM), the world's leading website for accurate Holocaust information.

Some of the events in this book are hard to read about. I've been guided by the words of Chella Velt Meekcoms Kryszek, who never shied from telling young people about her experiences as a teen during the Holocaust. "'I want you to be upset about it because I want you to think about what I am telling you,'" she said.

I also continue to be inspired by the life of Niels Skov, whom I met and wrote about in *Courage & Defiance: Stories of Spies, Saboteurs, and Survivors in World War II Denmark*. In Denmark (which is not covered here), a growing wave of resistance led ordinary people to thwart the Nazis' plans to deport Denmark's 7,000 Jews. But in 1940, when Niels first began to defy his Nazi oppressors, he did so on his own—entirely alone.

Recalling this, Niels said, "Swim against the stream. Don't do what everyone else does." Some of the partisans, resistance fighters, and rescuers you'll read about here did just that: They fought against the current, taking great risks to evade, resist, and defy evil and oppression.

"Like history, life continues," wrote Danish historian Jacob Presser, himself a Holocaust survivor. He added, "But sometimes there must be one who remembers."

World War II is now history, but it didn't happen so long ago. (In fact, I am writing these words on September 3, 2019, the eightieth anniversary of the official start of World War II.) I've included links so you can listen to or watch interviews with some of the survivors whose stories are included here. Many shared their experiences to honor loved ones murdered during the Holocaust: to give the dead a voice.

Their testimonies also serve as a call to action, a reminder that it's up to us to work for a world where genocide is unthinkable. But we don't have to be larger-than-life heroes or in the middle of war to practice being fair, just, inclusive, and kind—to stand up for someone else.

The work of making that world begins in the here and now, in ordinary, everyday actions. It begins with us.

—Deborah Hopkinson

CONTENTS

Part Three

DESPERATION AND DEFIANCE
True Stories from Poland

PART ONE

Fleeing from Evil, Hiding from Horror

True Stories from Germany and the Netherlands

It is important to me to chronicle the events as they pertained to our lives under [the] Nazi regime during WWII.

Those of us that managed to survive the years of murder, terror and destruction are the last direct link to the Holocaust—an era in the history of mankind that must never be forgotten—only then can we be sure that it will never happen again.

—**FRED P. ANGRESS,** *Holocaust survivor*

I had an open look on life and was surrounded by not-Jewish friends who offered to help me. Because you would not even dare ask a thing like that.

This was not giving you something; this was sharing with you your doomed destination. Who would ask anything from anybody, that big?

—**FLORA BADER,** *Holocaust survivor*

Baldur von Schirach (saluting), leader of the Hitler Youth, and Julius Streicher (in light-colored jacket), editor of the antisemitic newspaper *Der Stürmer*, review a parade of Hitler Youth in Nuremberg, Germany, in 1933. By 1936, all Aryan German youth were expected to join.

ABOUT THE PEOPLE IN PART ONE

FRED (FRITS) P. ANGRESS was fourteen when he fled Berlin, Germany, in 1937 with his parents and two brothers. They settled in the Netherlands, hoping to be safe from Nazi persecution in a country that had remained neutral in World War I. Soon after Germany invaded the Netherlands in May of 1940, the Nazis began to target Jews. Fred tried to use his job with the Jewish Council to save others, but when the last raids loomed, hiding was his only chance.

EVA LAUFFER DEUTSCHKRON married Martin Deutschkron in 1939 in Berlin, Germany, when she was just twenty. Eva and Martin and their families tried desperately to escape before war trapped them and millions of other Jewish families in Nazi-occupied countries. They couldn't get out. When the secret police came looking for the young couple, they made a risky decision: to hide in Berlin, under the noses of the Nazis.

CHELLA VELT MEEKCOMS KRYSZEK was born in the Netherlands in 1928, just weeks before Anne Frank, whose diary of living in hiding has been read by millions. Like the Franks, the Velt family decided to go into hiding. Even with the support of the Dutch underground, no one in hiding was safe and the Velt family was captured. In the following months, sixteen-year-old Chella and her sister, Flora, faced unimaginable horrors, but somehow survived together. (Chella was married twice; her married names were Meekcoms and Kryszek. Here we'll use her maiden name of Velt.)

GERTRUD MICHELSOHN SONNENBERG lived with her younger sister, Herta, and their parents in Germany. In December of 1941, the Michelsohn family was deported from the city of Hanover to the Riga ghetto in Latvia, where living conditions were desperately hard. As more and more Jews were rounded up and taken away, Gertrud and Herta fought to stay alive.

KEY DATES IN PART ONE

1933 Hitler becomes chancellor of Germany.

1935 The Nuremberg Laws strip German Jews of their citizenship and impose other restrictions.

1938 November 9–10 sees an outbreak of widespread, organized violence targeting Jews. Jewish synagogues are burned and businesses and homes are ransacked and destroyed during Kristallnacht (Night of Broken Glass). Up to 30,000 Jewish men are arrested and imprisoned in concentration camps.

1939 On September 1, Germany invades Poland; because of its prior commitment to protect Poland, Great Britain declares war on Germany on September 3.

In the Netherlands, Westerbork camp is established. Initially it serves as a detention center for Jewish refugees coming into the country illegally.

1940 On May 10, Germany attacks neutral Holland (the Netherlands), which surrenders on May 14.

1941 German Jews in the Netherlands are declared stateless. The Germans establish a Jewish Council to carry out Nazi regulations. After some young Jews are deported on February 22–23, Dutch workers strike in protest on February 25–26.

1942 In the spring of 1942, Jews in the Netherlands and in Belgium are required to wear the Star of David. (This requirement, which was used to segregate, intimidate, and deport Jewish citizens, had gone into effect in September of 1941 for all Jews over age six in the Reich, including Germany, Austria, and annexed territories such as western Poland.)

More deportations take place in the summer of 1942. The Nazis enlarge Westerbork and use it as a transit center before deporting Jews to killing centers in the east, in Nazi-occupied Poland.

1943 Deportations continue and the last raid takes place on September 29, 1943. The Jewish Council is disbanded.

1945 On April 12, 1945, Westerbork camp is liberated. Hitler commits suicide on April 30. On May 7, Germany surrenders, to take effect the next day. VE Day (Victory in Europe Day) is celebrated on May 8.

Chapter One

EVA AND MARTIN: THEY SHALL NOT GET US ALIVE

HIDING IN BERLIN

Once we were in hiding there was no going back.

One day in 1934, a young Berlin teen named Eva Lauffer was walking down the street with her friend Emily. As a group of men carrying the Nazi flag came toward them, the teens pretended to look in a store window display. They were Jewish, and didn't want to salute the flag with the expected "Heil Hitler!" greeting.

Suddenly, one man broke away, ran up to the girls, and slapped them hard in the face. The message was clear: Under the Third Reich and Hitler's Nazi Party (National Socialist German Workers' Party), any act of defiance carried a risk—and a price.

After that day, Eva and her friend Emily made a resolution. They might not be able to risk defiance, but they didn't have to comply either. They decided that whenever they spotted a group of Nazis marching with a flag, they'd simply turn around and walk in the other direction or slip into a building out of sight.

"Because we absolutely refused to greet the flag," Eva declared.

Eva Lauffer Deutschkron was born on November 12, 1918, in Posen, Germany (now Poznan, Poland). More than sixty years later, in September of 1980, she shared her story with the Wisconsin Historical Society. It was a long interview—seven hours over two days. (At the end of this chapter and in the back, there's a link so you can hear Eva's voice.)

Eva's story is unusual: As a young woman she survived the Holocaust in Berlin, Germany, the epicenter of Nazi power. She and her husband, Martin Deutschkron, lost everyone they loved, except for each other. Their harrowing ordeal shows us how Hitler's Nazi regime relentlessly tore families apart in their pursuit of one goal: the eradication of the Jewish population of Europe.

THE BEGINNING

Eva was fourteen in the spring of 1933, when Adolf Hitler became chancellor of Germany, bringing the Nazi Party into power and launching a regime known as the Third Reich.

Eva's father died shortly before she was born, and her widowed mother, Hedwig, moved to Berlin with Eva and her older brother, Heinz. Eva's mother married Richard Hirschhahn; in 1927, Ruth was born. Ruth was nine years younger than Eva. The baby of the family, sweet Ruth became everyone's favorite.

Eva's parents tried to protect their children from the antisemitism that followed the Nazi Party's rise to power. But, like Nazi flags on the street, it was nearly impossible to avoid. The spring of 1933 saw book burnings of Jewish authors and a major boycott of Jewish businesses. Members of Hitler's storm troopers unit, called brownshirts or SA (short for *Sturmabteilung*), stormed through cities and towns, sowing fear and violence.

Although the term *antisemitism* was first used in 1879 to describe the persecution of people of Jewish faith and heritage, discrimination against Jews dates back thousands of years. Jews have often been wrongly blamed and

Nazis carrying flags march down a street while members of the League of German Girls stand on the sidewalk and salute. As a Jewish teenager in Berlin, Eva Lauffer Deutschkron refused to salute the flag.

made scapegoats for problems in society. Hitler and his followers tapped into age-old stereotypes and further argued that Jews were subhuman, inferior to people of Aryan, or Nordic, heritage. Antisemitism, as well as other forms of religious and racial prejudice, still exists in the twenty-first century. In fact, in November 2019, the Anti-Defamation League conducted a global survey that found an increase in antisemitic attitudes in several countries; there have also been violent attacks on Jews in the United States.

Eva felt the changes everywhere. Many of her non-Jewish friends joined the Hitler Youth group and began to exclude Eva. Some bullied her or had flimsy, manipulative excuses for their cruel words and actions. "'I can't see you anymore. I'm in the Hitler *Jugend* [Hitler Youth] now . . .' one girl told Eva. 'They would throw me out and you wouldn't want me to be thrown out.'"

In Vienna, Austria, pedestrians view a large Nazi sign posted on a restaurant window informing the public that this business is run by an organization of the National Socialist Party and Jews aren't welcome. Anschluss, the annexation of Austria by Germany, took place on March 12, 1938. Anschluss brought an escalation of the persecution of Jews in Austria.

HITLER AND ANTISEMITISM

Adolf Hitler, born in 1889 in Austria, had set out his antisemitic ideas in the first volume of his political autobiography, *Mein Kampf* ("My Struggle"), published in 1926. As he pursued his ambition of becoming führer, or leader, Hitler roused angry crowds. He promoted hatred and a racist philosophy in which Aryans, or non-Jewish Caucasians with white skin, fair hair, and blue eyes, were a superior race.

These ideas were promoted by German teachers in classrooms. Ruth David, who grew up in a German village, remembered being "taught" about racial characteristics. "Jews could not be 'Aryan,' however good, upright, blond, blue-eyed, etc. There were regular school classes on racial characteristics. Heads and noses were measured, color of eyes examined, and contrasting pictures shown of singularly ugly Jews and outstandingly handsome 'Aryans.'" Her teachers didn't hesitate to encourage students to look down on Jews.

Hitler also fueled resentment against Jews in Germany's struggling post–World War I economy. Jews had lived in Germany for generations; many Jewish men had fought and been decorated in World War I. Jewish people held important positions in universities, banking, publishing, and business.

But the 1929 crash of the United States stock market, ushering in the Great Depression, had worldwide impact. It was especially devastating in Germany because the 1919 Treaty of Versailles, which ended World War I, imposed steep financial reparations on Germany.

Ordinary Germans were looking for someone to blame, and Hitler was adept at stirring up frustration, resentment, and anger. In rally after rally as his Nazi Party gained power during the 1930s, Hitler fueled the notion that Jews were the cause of the country's problems, tapping into centuries of antisemitism.

Under Hitler, Jews suffered increasing persecution throughout the 1930s. They were fired from universities and other civil service positions, children were forbidden from attending public schools, people lost their businesses. Restrictions increased. The letter *J* was stamped on Jewish passports. Women were required to add the name Sarah to their own name, and men had to add the name Israel. Then, on November 9, 1938, these persecutions erupted into a night of horrifying violence.

TURNING POINT: KRISTALLNACHT

Beginning on November 9 (and in some cases spilling over into the next day), Nazis unleashed surprise attacks on Jews throughout Germany, Austria, and part of Czechoslovakia. Gangs of Nazi thugs destroyed over 1,000 synagogues and broke windows of 7,500 Jewish-owned businesses.

The stated rationale for Kristallnacht, the Night of Broken Glass, was retaliation for the murder of a German official by a young Jewish man angry about his family's deportation. The attacks on Jewish places of worship, homes, and businesses were

Local residents watch as flames consume the synagogue in Opava, now part of the Czech Republic. The synagogue was set on fire during Kristallnacht in November of 1938. Many places of worship burned to the ground as firefighters acted only to protect nearby buildings.

followed by the arrest and detention of thousands of Jewish men.

According to the USHMM, "Hundreds died in the camps as a result of the brutal treatment they endured. Most did obtain release over the next three months on the condition that they begin the process of emigration from Germany. Indeed, the effects of Kristallnacht would serve as a spur to the emigration of Jews from Germany in the months to come."

Today, historians sometimes point to Kristallnacht as the start of the Holocaust. It was a clear and dire warning to the Jewish community: No Jewish citizen was safe from the Nazis.

Kristallnacht galvanized the people of Great Britain into action to protect the most vulnerable: children. The British government launched an effort called the Kindertransport, or children's transport. The hastily organized program managed to get approval from Nazi officials to waive normal visa requirements and bring close to 10,000 Jewish children from Germany, Austria, and Czechoslovakia to safety. Most went by train to the Netherlands, then by boat to England. At

A man surveys the damage to the Lichtenstein leather goods store in Berlin, Germany, after the Kristallnacht pogrom, a violent attack on Jews.

the time, organizers assumed it would be a temporary separation. In the end, the majority of children who left home and found refuge in England never saw their parents again.

Eva's family felt the full brunt of the Kristallnacht attacks. Nazis shattered the windows of their clothing store and broke windows in the family's apartment. Luckily, Eva, Ruth, and their parents had gone to stay with relatives elsewhere in the city.

Eva's mother left on a trip to the United States right about this time; she'd managed to get a temporary visa to attend Eva's brother's graduation from college in Wisconsin. Eva's stepfather, a veteran of World War I, tried to stay out of sight. Badly shaken by the surprise

Jewish men, who have been rounded up for arrest in the days after Kristallnacht, are escorted down a street by German police and SA members in November of 1938.

attacks, he hoped to avoid arrest. That left Eva to deal with all the broken glass and other damage. "I had to go out, make all the arrangements, take care of it all, and clean it all up."

EVA AND MARTIN

After Kristallnacht, Jewish families accelerated their efforts to escape the Nazi regime. Hoping to leave together, Eva wed Martin Deutschkron, in May of 1939, a few months before her twenty-first birthday. Eva and Martin wanted to be married so they could emigrate together, and the newlyweds and their families continued to search for a way out.

Eva's brother, Heinz, was already safe in Madison, Wisconsin, where he'd remained after graduation. Heinz wanted to bring the rest of the family to the United States, but immigration required mounds of paperwork and long waits. There were quotas, or limits, on the number of visas available to Jews. Immigrants to the United States also needed an affidavit (a required document where a sponsor assumes financial responsibility for the immigrant).

In the end, like thousands upon thousands of others, Eva's family simply couldn't get out in time. On September 1, 1939, Germany invaded Poland. Great Britain had agreed to support Poland if it was invaded. When Germany refused to withdraw its troops, Great Britain acted. On Sunday, September 3, 1939, Great Britain declared war on Germany. World War II had begun.

THE STRUGGLE TO ESCAPE

"We were fighting for our life . . ." said Eva about this desperate time. "We had tried to get to America; we had tried to see if we can't get smuggled out of Germany. And one time [1939 or 1940] we came very close to it . . . Martin was supposed to be a wounded man, and I was supposed to be dressed up as his nurse, and we wanted to go over the border to Switzerland this way. We didn't do it. We got cold feet the last minute, and I don't think we would have made it."

When war broke out, the door to immigration slammed shut. Like so many other Jewish families, Eva and Martin were left to focus on trying to survive one day at a time.

"By this time we were in total tumult inside ourselves," said Eva. There was a feeling of despair and helplessness. "You were so involved in your everyday survival and the news and the badgering of the Jews was done so furiously that you just didn't know what was next. I mean, your liberties were taken, your food was shortened to a point where you came near starvation, and it was just a steady battle."

THEIR COURAGE WAS BROKEN

Things only got worse. At the end of October of 1942, the Nazis arrested Martin's parents. Eva's parents and her fifteen-year-old sister, Ruth, were also taken. Eva's parents, who had lost their store, were later released only because they were doing forced labor, sewing uniforms for the German military.

Desperate to save Ruth, the family tried to bribe a German official to take her off the transport train. It didn't work. Neither Martin's parents nor Ruth were seen again. (Records show that Ruth was deported to the Riga ghetto in Latvia, where she died at age fifteen.)

Ruth's family was devastated. "This was the end of their strength," Eva said of her heartbroken parents. "She was a darling of everybody. My husband loved her dearly and we all tried to spoil her."

For a while, Eva still held out some hope. Like many others, she and her family hadn't yet realized the full extent of the Holocaust. "We knew there were labor camps," said Eva. "We knew they existed and we knew that when people were strong enough and could work hard enough, we thought they had a chance to survive. You just had to work for Hitler. . . .

"When my sister was taken away we still in the beginning thought—we were very worried because she was not such a strong youngster, but we still thought maybe she would survive," said Eva. But before long she started hearing rumors about other, unimaginable places, camps "where people got just murdered."

THE FINAL SOLUTION

Nazi Germany began implementing the policy to kill all Jews, known as the "Final Solution" to the "Jewish question," following the Wannsee Conference, which was held in a Berlin suburb called Wannsee on January 20, 1942. The meeting included senior government officials and the SS, or *Schutzstaffel*. The SS was the elite secret police organization in charge of the system of concentration camps and killing centers.

Reinhard Heydrich, who chaired the event, was a key figure in organizing Kristallnacht and an architect of the Holocaust. While ideas about the Final Solution had been in the works since the summer of 1941, at Wannsee, outlines of the plan to deport Jews to extermination camps in occupied Poland took formal shape. According to the USHMM, between 1933 and 1945, the Nazis established more than 44,000 different camps, resulting in the deaths of six million innocent Jewish people in a systematic, ruthless campaign of state-sponsored murder.

The Final Solution was not the result of a single decision by Hitler. As Holocaust scholar Nikolaus

Wachsmann notes, "Instead, the Holocaust was the culmination of a dynamic murderous process, propelled by increasingly radical initiatives from above and below. During World War II, the Nazi pursuit of a Final Solution moved from increasingly lethal plans for Jewish 'reservations' to immediate extermination."

In addition to Jews, Nazi Germany killed Soviet and Polish citizens, Roma, people with disabilities, homosexuals, and others. Unfortunately, no single document lists all victims. Many families tried for years to discover where and how their loved ones were murdered.

Eva Lauffer Deutschkron's parents sewed military uniforms as part of forced labor. In the same way, Eva was made to work at a munitions factory. Here, Jews at forced labor sew military uniforms for the German army and air force at a factory in the Olkusz [Krakow] ghetto in Poland in 1942.

A CLOSE CALL

Like her parents, Eva had been pressed into forced labor. Her job at the Siemens Munitions Factory outside Berlin gave her some protection from being deported, at least for a time. "I was making ammunition. We were not supposed to be taken until the very last minute," Eva explained. "Anybody that was of use to them [the Nazis], they kept till the last minute, and made life more and more difficult, as difficult as they could."

Her reprieve didn't last. One day in January of 1943, Nazi officials appeared at their apartment building and informed the janitor (the resident caretaker) they were there to pick up Eva and Martin Deutschkron.

"Our apartment was on the fourth floor, and our janitor was against Hitler," said Eva. So while the men waited upstairs for Eva and Martin, the janitor kept watch. When she saw Martin coming home from his tailoring job, she pulled him into her own apartment to warn him. Martin's first thoughts were for Eva.

"So he went then to my parents and told my parents that the Gestapo [state secret police] is there to take us," said Eva, "and they said, 'Let's see that we get Eva, that she doesn't get into their hands.'"

While Eva's parents went to the train station, Martin set off to meet Eva at work. Even that was dangerous.

Since he didn't have the needed permit to ride the train to her factory, Martin had to remove the identifying Star of David he was supposed to wear. Luckily, when Eva came out of work after her shift, she spotted Martin at once.

"I saw him standing there without a star; I knew something was wrong. Because you had to have special permit to use the train as a Jew and [if] you lived farther than seven miles away you got a permit to ride the train, but only from and to work. So I had this permit; he didn't have it. So he couldn't, with a Jewish star, get on the train to come."

Eva walked past him without a word. "I couldn't go up to him because I would have given him away. So I got on the train and he got on the same train and we rode back and at the railroad station there was my mother standing, a little farther over at the corner there was my father standing. They were so afraid—if one would miss me, the other one would see me."

GO OUT AND FIGHT FOR YOUR LIFE

Martin and Eva spent the night at her parents' apartment. The next morning, Eva's parents told them, "'You are young. You go out and fight for your life. You have nothing to lose. They take you now, you get killed. If they catch you, you get killed, too, but at least don't go without a fight.'"

Martin had come to the same decision. "'They shall not get us alive.'"

It was January of 1943; the war had been raging for more than three years. Martin and Eva hoped they might need to live in hiding for only a few months. The reality turned out to be far different. The young couple stayed on the run, moving from one temporary hiding place to another until the end of the war in Europe, in May of 1945.

Since they had contacts in the clothing industry and tailoring, they looked there first for help. Martin was able to find a place with a Hungarian tailor named Franz Gomber who gave him sewing work and a place to stay, though Martin had to fashion a bed from an ironing board. Eventually, Eva went to stay with Franz too.

"He was not Jewish, but he was against Hitler," said Eva. Franz used the money Martin earned sewing to buy food for them on the black market.

But Franz was often careless about the dangers involved in hiding Eva and Martin and didn't take proper precautions to protect them. He liked to invite friends over to gamble and play cards. One evening, a card player spied the flame of a heating plate in the other room and said, "'You are hiding somebody there.'"

Fortunately, the man wasn't an informer. Instead, he

offered to help the couple get false identification documents in exchange for Martin making him a suit. In this way, Eva and Martin got their first false identity papers, which were essential if they were to pass as non-Jewish Germans.

"Martin became Franz Erich Gebhardt," said Eva. As a young man, Martin was at a special risk of being stopped, since he would be expected to be a soldier. In this case, Martin's false papers showed that he had been discharged from the military for medical reasons. Eva had a different name as well.

But just getting papers wasn't enough. Since Martin's papers were related to a military discharge, they required regular official date stamps to remain authentic. When another card player named Videk Kauser found out about the couple, he agreed to help. When Martin showed him the identity paper, the man said, "'I work in this department and you come to me and I'll put the legal stamp on it. . . . Don't worry . . . you'll be safe.'"

Could he be trusted? And would Martin actually dare to walk into a Nazi office? They decided to take the risk. "So Martin really went—you can imagine how scared he was," said Eva. Not only was Videk Kauser true to his word, he tried to help Eva and Martin by making them a meal Eva never forgot—in more ways than one.

"And this fellow felt very sorry for us and invited us to his house for a good meal," recalled Eva. And so they went. "I remember until today; I still see them in front of me. He had potato pancakes, golden brown, fried in butter.

"We got so violently ill we thought we'd die, because we were undernourished. But I've never forgotten him. . . . He did a great deed for us by helping us with these papers."

Although Eva and Martin had trusted this one man, they lived in a constant state of alert. Informers were everywhere; one mistake or false step could mean their arrest and death.

And it soon seemed the Nazis were closing in on them: The man who'd procured their first false identity papers was caught. Next, Franz, the tailor hiding them, was brought in for questioning. It was too dangerous to stay: The apartment could be searched at any moment.

Eva and Martin turned to a series of helpers: friends, cousins, and old work acquaintances. Sometimes people turned them away, unwilling to risk their own safety. At other times, help came from unexpected allies.

Once, an old family acquaintance who worked for the Gestapo, or secret state police, which fell under the jurisdiction of the SS, helped Eva sneak back into her empty apartment to fetch some extra clothes. It was dangerous. The apartment had been sealed, so any small noise was bound to rouse the suspicion of the Nazi sympathizers who lived in the apartment just below.

They went in the middle of the night. Eva tiptoed around quietly. Suddenly, a coat hanger slipped from her hand and clattered on the floor. Eva and her helper had to rush out of the building.

There were times when Eva and Martin ran out of options and were left totally on their own. Eva recalled one stormy, harrowing night in a suburb of Berlin when they had nowhere to sleep. They dared not stay in one place very long for fear of being questioned. "So we went from a telephone booth to the railroad station in the rain all night long. . . . We made it through the night."

Anxious to keep in touch with her parents, Eva had snuck out to meet them once a week at a cousin's house. One day they didn't show up. Their apartment was now sealed too, a sign that the family who lived there was gone. Eva never saw them again. Records show they were deported to Auschwitz in March of 1943 and did not survive.

And so it went, day by day, week by week, month after month. From January of 1943, when they first went into hiding, until the end of the war, Eva and Martin never had one safe, permanent hiding place. Sometimes it seemed as though bad luck stalked them. Once, they moved into a basement apartment posing as the niece and nephew of the building's caretakers. Just after they moved in, the building was hit in an Allied bombing raid and they had to pull each other out of the wreckage. Mistaken for non-Jewish refugees of the bombed-out building, Eva and Martin were given food rationing cards for a week of supplies.

They went next to a fellow tailor who lived on the outskirts of Berlin with his wife and daughters. Mr. Peltzer didn't tell his wife who these guests really were. Only Mr. Peltzer knew the truth: that Eva and Martin were Jews in hiding. He let them sleep on the porch. Sometimes they spent the days hiding in the woods. Other days, they risked going into Berlin to do tailoring jobs in someone's apartment to earn enough to buy food on the black market or directly from farmers.

SO PEACEFUL AND STILL SO TERRIBLE

In the summer of 1944, Martin made friends with a farm family near the Peltzers who agreed to lend them a room while they worked as tailors in Berlin. Eva treasured this rare, brief interlude of peace. "I remember that I felt like in a cloud. They had these down quilts, you know, on the bottom the down quilt, you slept in it and on top also the down quilt. In the morning we would walk to the train to take it into Berlin. . . .

"I remember us walking across the fields. It was so peaceful, and we were so upset and so torn . . ." she said of one beautiful sunrise. "I remember this horrible impact it left on me. How can the world be so peaceful and still so terrible?"

Before long, though, a local policeman noticed the couple and began asking questions. That hiding place became too dangerous. So they returned to live on the porch of the Peltzer house.

Martin's false papers were now obsolete, so he stayed on the property, chopping wood and doing chores during the day. As the tide of war shifted, Allied bombing raids in the Berlin area intensified. Martin made himself useful by helping the family build a makeshift bomb shelter in their yard. Still, it was an uneasy situation; Mr. Peltzer's wife became increasingly suspicious. Eva worried constantly that Mr. Peltzer might turn them in.

HE GOES WITH YOU

When Eva's mother had urged them to go out and fight, Eva had thought they might need to be in hiding for a few months. "Of course, nobody expected it to be two and a half years. And, of course, once we were in hiding there was no going back. So it was just going on from day to day to day," said Eva.

All they could do was hope for the end to come. "But it didn't come and didn't come and didn't come. And when it finally came we couldn't believe it was the end."

But even this time was fraught with danger. By the spring of 1945, Allied troops were advancing on Berlin. Eva and Martin realized they could easily get caught in the middle of a battlefield and decided to leave the area. Eva's friend Miriam, who'd also hidden in the countryside, came with them. It was a time of chaos and uncertainty. By now the entire Peltzer family knew the truth about Martin and Eva.

On the road, they encountered Russian Allied troops who were putting German men into receiving camps to be interrogated and held. At one military checkpoint, Martin was questioned separately from Eva and Miriam. Martin's papers, though out-of-date, still showed him as a German with a medical discharge from the military.

Could Martin prove he was a Jew in hiding? If he couldn't, the Russians might make him a prisoner of war. The next day, Eva and Miriam were told they could go; Martin was ordered to stay. Eva panicked at the thought of being separated.

"I started crying something terrible," remembered Eva. "And Miriam was trying to console me and Martin wasn't with us, they had kept him separate already. I said, 'We were together underground all this time and nobody separated us. Now the war is over and now we should get separated. We have no place that we would ever find each other again.'"

To Eva's astonishment, a Russian soldier who understood German overheard her—and believed her story. Not only that, he acted to help. He came over and whispered, "'Don't worry. I'll get you your husband. He goes with you.'"

And he did.

FACE EVERY MINUTE

Throughout the chaos and confusion at the end of the war, Eva and Martin stuck together. In May of 1946, shortly after their son, Edward, was born, they came to the United States. After living in New York City, they moved to Madison, Wisconsin, in 1948 to be close to Eva's brother. Their daughter, Ruth, named for Eva's sister, was born in 1952.

When asked how she had the strength to survive in hiding for so long, Eva said that it had been exhausting physically and emotionally. Although they were petrified, they tried never to show each other their fears. It would have made it harder. "We just lived from day to day," Eva said. "Faced every minute."

In Madison, Eva and Martin established a clothing and retail business called Martin's, Inc. They were married for nearly fifty years before Martin passed away in 1985. Eva died in 2011 at the age of ninety-two, living long enough to enjoy three grandchildren and four great-grandchildren.

Postwar portrait of Eva and Martin Deutschkron with their son, Edward, in Central Park, New York, in 1947.

LOOK, LISTEN, REMEMBER: You can see more photos of Eva, Martin, and their family over the years, and hear Eva's full story, by visiting the Wisconsin Historical Society's Holocaust Survivors Project: https://www.wisconsinhistory.org/HolocaustSurvivors /Deutschkron.asp.

Chapter Two

GERTRUD: HOLD YOURSELF TRUE AND STRONG

FROM GERMANY TO THE RIGA GHETTO IN LATVIA

Our hunger was so great we had no choice.

NO ONE WANTED TO KNOW US

"My sister Herta and I grew up in our early years like any other German children, in a town called Hausberge, or Porta Westfalica," begins Gertrud Michelsohn Sonnenberg's remarkable story of survival.

Gertrud was born in 1919, a year after Eva Deutschkron, and Herta came along in 1920. Like Eva, the sisters were young teens in the early years of the Nazi regime. They soon experienced bullying and antisemitism

Herta and Gertrud Michelsohn
(Sonnenberg) around 1921.

firsthand. "My sister and I were no longer allowed to answer in school, or to raise our hands," said Gertrud. "This was very hard on us, for we had grown up with the other children, and now no one wanted to know us anymore. That was the beginning."

Gertrud's parents suffered too. Her father owned a rock quarry. He lent money to a non-Jewish friend, but never got it back: The man claimed that he didn't need to repay the loan since Mr. Michelsohn was Jewish. Gertrud's father lost his business. The family then moved to the city of Hanover, where Gertrud's mother supported them by sewing.

The Michelsohns were forced to carry identification cards and wear the six-pointed Star of David, a symbol of Judaism. Gertrud had to stand in the back of trolley cars even when there were empty seats. She could only walk in the street, not on the sidewalk.

Yet, like many other German Jews, Gertrud's parents kept hoping the Nazis would fall out of power. They couldn't believe their country would completely turn against them. They were "Germans first and Jewish last. That's not surprising since they had been there for so many generations," explained Gertrud. "My father and uncle fought in World War I and received decorations. When my father finally saw the light, it was too late."

After war broke out on September 3, 1939, Gertrud and her family moved to an apartment and took in boarders. Then, in late 1941, everything changed.

BEING DEPORTED

"We were told to be prepared to be picked up at any time to go away, but they didn't tell us where," said Gertrud. "We were allowed 100 pounds per person for clothes. We could pack all our things, they told us, and they would ship it to us.

"We believed it. My mother packed her sewing machine."

Gertrud and her family were taken to a former Jewish school that served as a collection point. There were about a thousand other Jewish people there. They were made to stand all night, while SS officers searched them for gold and took away the clothing they'd brought along.

"Then they sent us in a transport to Riga, a town in Latvia. . . . They put us on a train, with a loaf of bread, a jar of water, and some sausage," said Gertrud. "We were very fortunate, for we were in a regular train, instead of cattle cars. . . . But on the last night, they took the locomotive away, and then we had no heat or light . . . We were in a desolate wilderness.

"We were forced to make a very long walk. It was bitterly cold. For whoever was not able to walk, we were told, there were buses. My mother had terrible asthma, and I told her to go on the bus, but she said she wouldn't leave us.

"Those bus transports never arrived at the camp. The people who had accepted rides were gassed right in the buses and put in open trenches."

THE RIGA GHETTO

Some deportation lists still exist. Thanks to the dedicated staff of the Leo Baeck Institute in New York, we have chilling evidence of the systematic removal of people from their homes and placement into ghettos and camps. And so we can see the names of Gertrud, Herta, and their parents, Frieda and Max Michelsohn, on a list of Jews deported from Hanover, Germany, to the Riga ghetto in Latvia, a country on the Baltic Sea, on December 15, 1941.

Ghettos were key elements in bringing about the "Final Solution," the Nazi policy to annihilate Jewish people. "The Germans saw the ghettos as a provisional measure to control and segregate Jews while the Nazi leadership in Berlin deliberated upon options for the removal of the Jewish population," notes the USHMM.

Ghettos were certain areas of cities and towns where Jews were required to live. Many were closed off by walls and patrolled by guards. Residents endured desperately crowded living conditions and had little access to food. When Gertrud and her family arrived, they saw starving, malnourished people in freezing weather. "We were told to go in any house . . . and we had to sleep with people we never knew."

Jewish councils and a police force enforced Nazi orders. These individuals came under the close scrutiny of their Nazi oppressors. "The Germans did not hesitate to kill those Jewish policemen who were perceived to have failed to carry out orders," notes the USHMM.

The police force was sometimes ordered to round up people in the ghetto for a further deportation, usually to one of six extermination camps established in Nazi-occupied Poland—Chelmno, Belzec, Sobibor, Treblinka, Auschwitz (a complex sometimes known as Auschwitz-Birkenau), and Majdanek. Extermination camps were killing centers. During the Holocaust, six million Jews—innocent children, women, and men—were murdered.

SHOVELING SNOW

Gertrud and her family arrived in the Riga ghetto in bitter cold. The ghetto was surrounded by a barbed wire fence. All around her, Gertrud saw people struggling to survive in horrific conditions. She was soon put to work.

"I was sent to shovel snow, which was a terrible occupation. Almost eight months out of every year, as it turned out, I had to shovel snow from six in the morning till dark," she said. "This is how most people got frozen hands or feet. We would stand on a bridge over the river, with the wind blowing on all sides. Lunch was only watery soup. The Germans wanted our labor, but it was also clear they wanted to work us to death."

Gertrud often shoveled in subzero weather without warm winter clothing. Her sister, Herta, who'd trained as a nurse, was assigned to the ghetto hospital. There she saw the results of these pitiless working conditions. Herta had to assist in amputations of frozen limbs, which was done without anesthesia. Gertrud remembered that the notorious commander of the camp, a cruel man named Kurt Krause, would sometimes watch these operations because he enjoyed seeing Jewish people suffer.

Daily life was a desperate struggle. Even so, Gertrud remembered that ghetto residents came together to form schools, an orchestra, a beauty parlor, and even a ballet group. There was a dark side to this too. "Whenever there was to be a slaughter, we were told to put on a performance. The SS would sit with us, all like one big family, and the next day they would kill us."

Yet there were also people who took risks to help, even in small ways. Gertrud said, "In all of the misery, you always met somebody who had a heart. I once cleaned for a couple of soldiers. One was so kind, he gave me his soap. He endangered his life, giving me his ration."

BE BRAVE

For nearly two years, Gertrud's family managed to survive in the Riga ghetto. On November 2, 1943, Gertrud's parents were ordered to go to a central collection point. Gertrud was working, but Herta went along with them. Gertrud's mother guessed what was about to happen.

"My mother told my sister to leave and stay with me instead," said Gertrud, "but Herta wanted to remain with my parents.

Even in ghettos or in hiding, children and teens continued their education whenever possible. Here, an open page of a book of English lessons handwritten in Dutch and English by Albert and Max Heppner while in hiding in Deurne-Zeilberg, Holland, in 1944–1945. Herb DeLevie (1934–1989), who went into hiding in the Netherlands at age seven, remembered the Dutch underground bringing thirty or forty books at a time to the farmhouse where he and his family were hidden. He estimated he read 3,000 books during the war as he tried to keep up his studies. An atlas came in especially useful. "You played games like naming the countries of the world and their capitals, the biggest river, the biggest mountains . . . these type of things." Herb also loved to draw and put that skill to good use. He survived and immigrated to the United States, where he became an architect.

"'You will need me,' she told them.

"At this point my mother told Herta she was freezing and asked her to fetch a jacket. When my sister returned, they were gone. That is how my mother saved her."

Before they were taken away, the girls' mother got

hold of a small piece of paper. Both parents scribbled a last message and asked a Jewish policeman to deliver it to their daughter.

"When I received the note that day, I was very confused and crumpled it up without reading it. I couldn't find my parents or my sister, and I really lost control," said Gertrud. "I wanted to kill myself, and I stood at a window ready to jump out."

Later, after she knew Herta was safe, Gertrud unfolded the paper again to read her parents' final words. Her mother told them she loved them, and urged her daughters to be brave. Her father wrote, "'Dear children, we do not know the destination of our journey, what will happen to us, we don't know. Be brave and hold yourself true and strong in all situations.'"

In the long, horrible months that followed, Gertrud kept the note in a small bag around her neck, along with a few photographs she'd saved. Once, after she talked back to a soldier, it was taken from her. She talked him into returning it to her.

Against incredible odds, Gertrud and Herta hung on. They endured the terrifying selections, when they were made to stand outside while the camp commander pointed to the right or left. By this time everyone knew that in one direction lay death.

The sisters did whatever they had to in order to get food. "We tried to sell our shirts and slips and other things to Latvian Christian women in exchange for butter and eggs," said Gertrud. "People were hanged for this. There were spot checks when we came back [into the ghetto] from work details, and those caught smuggling in food were killed . . . So we knew what we were doing, but we did it anyway. Our hunger was so great we had no choice."

On one bright day, Gertrud noticed the golden, onion-shaped domes of a nearby church. "The sun glinted off the gold, and the sky was so blue. How can people behave like animals, I used to think, when there is such beauty in the world?"

In the fall of 1944, Allied Soviet troops entered Latvia. Nearly all the Jews in the Riga ghetto had been killed. When the German soldiers were forced to retreat, they took the remaining Jews along with them. Gertrud and Herta became part of a group of about two hundred prisoners moved from here to there in the following months.

They went from a port on the Baltic Sea to a prison in Hamburg, Germany. From there, the Nazis forced them to walk about sixty miles to a town called Kiel-Hasse.

"There were SS all around us. Bombs were falling, and we slept in barns, among horses and sheep, to be warm."

At one point, Herta gave up, too exhausted to move. She sat on the side of the road. Gertrud and a friend joined her. Gertrud was panicking. "The SS were coming already, and it would have meant that we would all be shot. My sister looked at us and suddenly regained her senses."

Herta stood up and they kept going.

COUNT BERNADOTTE

And then something unexpected occurred. "During the walk a foreign-looking delegation pulled up and a man got out and asked the SS what kind of people we were. 'Just some left-over Jews,' they told him. 'We don't know what to do with them.'"

Gertrud later found out the man was Count Folke Bernadotte of Sweden, on his way to a meeting with Nazi official Heinrich Himmler to negotiate the release of prisoners in the closing days of the war. "He had been told that there were no more Jews in Germany, but he informed Himmler that he had seen us, and he asked for us as part of an exchange."

At the time, of course, Gertrud and Herta knew nothing about any of this. They were forced to keep on their death march to Kiel-Hasse. How it would have ended, Gertrud would never know. But she felt sure Count Bernadotte's intervention had saved them. "Had Count Bernadotte not come for us when he did, there would not have been anybody left alive."

And then one night, the prisoners were awakened by their guards and pushed outside. To her astonishment, Gertrud saw vehicles with red crosses lined up waiting.

At first, no one believed it could be true. Were they really to be saved?

"They practically had to push us into the vans with their guns," said Gertrud. The prisoners rode in the dark for hours.

The vans stopped and they were counted. Then word came that they were approaching the border with Denmark. "'When the doors open again, you will be free,'" the guards told them.

"We didn't believe it. But it was true."

It was May of 1945, in the final days of the war. Gertrud and Herta had survived.

In Denmark, Gertrud and Herta were given showers, clothes, and food—too much food! "We were people who hadn't had regular food in four years, but they gave us sardines, cookies, chocolate—a big package for every two people. We ate it all, in one shot."

The group was then put on a train for the harbor, to take a boat to Sweden for medical treatment. Since everyone was so malnourished, the rich food they'd eaten made them violently ill—so ill the train had to be stopped and cleaned. Everyone got showers again too.

Gertrud had blood poisoning in her arm, which nearly had to be amputated. It took a year for her to heal and recuperate from her long ordeal. "We were nursed back to health by the Swedes. . . . After we were ready, they provided each of us a job in our own profession, or as close to it as they could manage. And they gave us living quarters, and some money for food. And then we were on our own."

WE LEARNED TO BE SILENT

Gertrud and Herta stayed in Sweden for three and a half years before immigrating to the United States. "In the beginning, we wanted to talk of our experiences to people in America, but we found that no one wanted to listen. 'Start life over,' they told us. 'Don't think about the past.' It was hard for us not to speak of what we had witnessed and what we had lived through.

"It really hurt us. But we learned to be silent."

In 1980, Gertrud and her husband, along with Herta, returned to Hanover, Germany, at the invitation of that city. Gertrud was able to visit her birthplace and speak with others from her past. The Jewish policeman who brought Gertrud the note from her parents also survived the war.

Fortunately, Gertrud did not remain silent about her experiences. In 1985, she told her story to writer Enid Bloch; it was published in the newsletter of Gertrud's temple in Bridgewater, New Jersey. A copy was also given to the Leo Baeck Institute in New York to be preserved for readers in the future. Gertrud and Herta married and lived in New Jersey with their families. Gertrud passed away in 2003 and Herta in 2006.

LOOK, LISTEN, REMEMBER: You can watch a video interview with Gertrud Sonnenberg by searching "Gertrud Sonnenberg" at the United States Holocaust Memorial Museum at https://www.ushmm.org/ or by following this link: https://collections.ushmm.org/search/catalog/irn505503.

Chapter Three

FRED: I BECAME PART OF THEIR FAMILY

RESISTANCE AND HIDING IN AMSTERDAM

If you want to stay alive you have to go into hiding.

Fred Angress was born Fritz Peter Angress on April 14, 1923. Fred was one of three boys: His brother Werner was three years older; Hans Herbert five years younger. Werner liked to call his middle brother *Möpschen*, or Little Pug Nose.

Fred was ten when the Third Reich began. "My brothers and I attended public schools and until Hitler came to power in 1933, we never considered ourselves to be different from anyone else," he said. "However, things began to change rapidly. It did not take long for Hitler to ingrain prejudice and hate against the Jews in the minds of the German citizens."

Fred said, "Some of my former classmates, kids I had considered to be my friends, started to harass me and called me a 'Dirty Jew.'" When a law passed forbidding Jewish children to attend public schools, Fred and his brothers switched to Jewish schools.

And, of course, Nazi flags flew everywhere. Fred's brother Werner recalled that the streets became seas of flags. In his own small act of defiance, Werner hung the former imperial flag of Germany on their balcony, and also fastened a flag pennant to his bicycle. He kept it on his bike until the day an elderly gentleman stopped him on the street and advised him to replace it with a Nazi swastika. Werner removed it, but the flag on the balcony stayed put.

Like so many other Jewish families, the Angresses kept hoping things would get better. "Later in the United States, I was often asked why we didn't pack up and leave the country immediately after the Nazis took power in 1933. If we had known what was in store for us, my family and probably the majority of German Jews would have done just that," wrote Werner. "But of course we didn't know. . . . We waited, tried to adjust, hoped the Nazis would change their minds about the

Jews, and otherwise went about our daily activities at work, at home, and at school."

There were also powerful reasons to stay. The boys' father, Ernst Angress, a successful banker, was hesitant to abandon his career and the success he'd achieved. "Papa was reluctant to take his wife and children to a foreign country, where his future would have been uncertain," Werner explained. "As long as the business was doing alright—and until 1937 that was the case—my parents refused to emigrate, in spite of the steadily increasing gravity of the regime's policies toward the Jews."

Three young Jewish boys care for a cow at the Gross Breesen agricultural training center, sometime between 1936 and 1938. Fred Angress's brother Werner lived at this farm for a time.

But as his sons grew, Mr. Angress began to worry about their future prospects in Nazi Germany. In May of 1936, to give Werner more options, his dad sent him to the Gross Breesen Training Farm for Emigrants, an agricultural training program. There, Werner could acquire practical skills to improve his chances of being accepted as an immigrant by another country.

FLIGHT!

Werner loved the farm, but less than eighteen months later, in October of 1937, his father summoned him home unexpectedly. Mr. Angress had changed his mind. He wanted to escape Germany with the entire family while they still could.

Fred, his brother Hans, and their mother went first to England, staying in London for several months. Meanwhile, Mr. Angress, worried about supporting his family, made a fateful decision—to smuggle his savings out of the country even though this was illegal. While emigration for Jews was still allowed at this time, families were forbidden from bringing their wealth with them.

Through a contact, Fred's father got a chance to invest in a shop selling women's lingerie in Amsterdam, so the family moved to the Netherlands. (While the correct name for the entire country is the Netherlands, people sometimes refer to it as Holland. Technically, Holland applies to two provinces; Amsterdam is in North Holland.)

At first all went well. "I remember the years between 1938 and 1940 as being the happiest of my life as a

Like Fred's family, Anne and Margot Frank and their parents fled Germany for the Netherlands in the 1930s. Here, Anne and Margot pose with childhood friends in February of 1934 (possibly for Margot's eighth birthday or a Jewish holiday gathering). Pictured from left to right are: unknown; Anne Frank (front row left); Evelyn Werthauer; Barbara Ledermann Rodbell; unknown; Margot Frank (back row right).

Margot was in the same class as Barbara Ledermann Rodbell, who was born in Berlin and arrived in Amsterdam with her family in 1933. Her family became friends with the Franks. Barbara, a dancer, joined the Jewish resistance. Like Otto Frank, Anne and Margot's father, she was the sole survivor of her family. Her parents and sister were deported and murdered at Auschwitz. She moved to the United States in 1947. Barbara is featured in the PBS film *Daring to Resist*, about three Jewish teens during the war.

teenager. Holland was a beautiful country, there was a surplus of food and the business did well," said Fred. After finishing school, Fred worked in the family store.

Meanwhile, thanks to his time at the training farm, Werner was able to get a visa for the United States. On October 28, 1939, a friend drove Werner and his parents to Rotterdam, where Werner would take a train to Antwerp to board a ship across the Atlantic.

Werner never forgot their parting. "My parents tried hard to smile as they hugged me. With a pounding heart I got on the train and waved to them from the window. It was the last time I saw my father, standing by the car, waving to me."

Werner couldn't know that when he next saw his mother and brothers, he'd be a master sergeant in the United States Army.

A SURPRISE ATTACK

A few months later, on May 10, 1940, the Angress family awoke to find the Netherlands under siege. They'd fled Germany for safety. Now there were German soldiers in the streets. "I remember it vividly," said Fred, who was then seventeen. "It was early on a Friday morning when we heard a news flash over the radio."

Amsterdam's airport had been attacked by German aircraft. "We were shocked—the attack by the Nazis was totally unexpected," Fred said. "A friend and I decided to bicycle to the airport to see if it was true, or mere propaganda. We were stopped midway by Dutch police who confirmed the attack and advised us to go home."

The Dutch were no match for the more powerful German forces, and the fighting lasted less than a week. Queen Wilhelmina and the Dutch government fled to England in exile. The German occupation of the Netherlands had begun.

"We made several attempts to get out of Holland, like so many others trying to escape the clutches of the Third Reich. People headed for the harbor and tried to sail to England," said Fred. "My father was given the chance to go there on a submarine, but the fear of having his family arrested prevented him from leaving. The Germans caught on fast. Guards were posted at the harbor and no one was allowed to leave the Netherlands."

WE ARE IN POWER NOW

The Netherlands was now being run by a German administration. Jews were soon forbidden to work in civil service or public positions. In 1941, Jews were required to register with the authorities and provide a name and address. Nearly 160,000 Jews registered, which included about 25,000 Jewish refugees from Germany—people like Fred and his family.

Since Fred's father had violated the law by moving his savings out of Germany, it was only a matter of time before he was caught. On April 25, 1941, two German officials from a financial department came to question him. They told Mr. Angress they'd be back to arrest him in twenty-four hours. Fred's father might have gone into hiding at that point, yet he feared this act of defiance would put his wife and sons in more danger.

Mr. Angress was arrested and sentenced to a year in prison, first in Amsterdam and then in Berlin. After her husband had served some months, Mrs. Angress went to speak to an official to ask about his safe return when his sentence was up. There was no chance of that, the official told her bluntly. "'Frau Angress, if YOU were in power now, you would kill US. However, now WE are in power and WE kill YOU.'"

Fred never saw his father again. Ernst Angress was transferred from Brandenburg Prison in Berlin to Auschwitz death camp in Poland, where he was murdered on January 19, 1943. The official cause of death was listed as heart failure.

ONLY A MIRACLE

In June of 1942, Fred received a letter saying he'd been given the "privilege" of working in the textile mills of

Germany to support the war effort. The letter said he'd stay first at Westerbork, a transit camp in the Netherlands near the German border. It also included a list of items he was supposed to pack.

Fred's family was immediately suspicious. There was still a lot of confusion about labor camps at this time, especially among Dutch families who'd always felt safe living in the Netherlands. A survivor named Flora Hony Bader (born in Amsterdam in 1919 as Flora Melkman) remembered that her brother went willingly to a labor camp because he believed he was strong enough to survive hard work.

"We Dutch Jews did absolutely not believe—even I, who had read *Mein Kampf* [Hitler's political autobiography that laid out his antisemitic beliefs]—that we would be killed. My greatest fear was that we would have to work and work very hard. That is as bad as I could think it would be," Flora explained.

"But when I saw the sick people go and old people, I was wondering, 'Why do they want those people to work? They cannot work.'"

Likewise, Fred's mother, who'd already lost her husband, feared for her son's safety. "But what could she do to protect me from the dangers of transportation to the unknown? Only a miracle could save me," said Fred.

A day or two before Fred was supposed to report to

the authorities, his mother had an appointment at a beauty salon. "She was terribly worried about me, and did not feel like going, but at the last moment decided not to cancel after all," Fred recalled. "Her decision to keep this appointment turned out to be a Godsend that saved my life."

At the beauty parlor, Fred's mother met a woman whose husband worked for the Jewish Council. Mrs. Angress pleaded with her, asking for a job for Fred to delay his deportation. In this way, Fred escaped being transported to Mauthausen death camp, where thousands were executed. Later, Fred reflected that not one of those who left on that transport survived.

SMUGGLING PEOPLE TO SAFETY

Fred's job with the Jewish Council gave him temporary exemption from being deported. As they did in other countries they occupied, the Germans established Jewish councils to carry out Nazi policies and orders, including deportations. Some people in Jewish councils committed suicide or resisted outright and were killed. Others tried to save as many people as possible by secretly subverting orders. The USHMM put it this way: "The members of the Jewish councils faced impossible moral dilemmas."

Fred was determined to use his own reprieve to help others. "We tried to sabotage the work of the Nazis whenever possible, smuggling out as many people as we could." Fred and other council workers wore special armbands. When they could, they tucked extra armbands in their pockets and put them on people who were already registered to be transported. They then walked out of the courtyard together past the guards.

Fred's Jewish Council office was in the same building as the SS (*Schutzstaffel*), the feared special police force and branch of Nazi operations responsible for concentration camps. Whenever he was working, Fred kept his eyes open—and one day it paid off.

"I happened to come across a batch of blank identification cards. I quickly took them and hid them in my clothing, praying that I would not be found out, and later handed them to the Dutch Underground which forged documents for those going into hiding."

Another time, he came across a list of Jews being paid by the

A Dutch Jew seeks assistance from the emigration department of the *Joodse Raad* (Jewish Council) in Amsterdam in 1942.

Nazis as informers. He carefully copied the names and warned everyone to stay clear of them. Fred's acts of resistance under the enemy's nose might have seemed small. Yet these actions saved lives. Most days he felt he was living in a den of lions. "The horrors we had hoped to leave behind when we fled Germany had caught up with us."

A DROP IN THE BUCKET

Sometimes Fred was assigned to an Amsterdam theater called the Hollandsche Schouwburg, which was used as a gathering place to assemble people for deportation. (Today it is the site of Holland's National Holocaust Memorial.) At first, Fred and others tried to smuggle people out of the building whenever the guard in the lobby happened to doze off. "But all our efforts amounted to just a drop in the bucket—we had to try to escalate the process."

A colleague and resistance activist named Walter Süskind came up with another scheme. "He would first treat the German SS guard to drinks, and then take the suicidal risk of arranging mass escapes . . . if caught he would have been shot instantly," Fred recalled. Six or seven Jewish Council members took part, each agreeing to lead small groups of six or more out of the building throughout the evening.

"One particular night stands out in my memory," said Fred. "I had gathered my six escapees around me and gave them instructions—to be absolutely quiet, not to talk and to tiptoe through the lobby and out the revolving door to (temporary) safety."

As Fred led the escapees into the lobby, another Jewish Council worker, a boisterous greengrocer, stood in front of the former ticket window, chatting with the SS guard and doing his best to distract him. The grocer was a large man, which helped to save the day.

One man following Fred was carrying a knapsack, to which he'd attached some pots and pans. "Just as I very quietly entered the lobby with my group, a string on the man's knapsack broke and all his pots and pans clattered to the tiled floor, making an unbelievable racket," said Fred. "My legs turned to rubber and I was unable to move, convinced that this was the end not only of our escape activities, but very probably of our lives.

"When I dared to look toward the ticket window, I couldn't believe it—our greengrocer had the full attention of the SS guard, who was laughing loudly at some joke and had completely missed the commotion."

Fred took a deep breath and got everyone out. Their luck had held.

Dutch Jews from the town of Hooghalen en route to Westerbork camp in October of 1942. Initially established in 1939 to house Jewish refugees who had entered the Netherlands illegally, Westerbork became a transit camp for Jews and Roma slated for deportation to death camps in Poland.

SAVING CHILDREN

Across from the Schouwburg theater, where people were gathered before being deported, there was a nursery school attached to a teachers' college. The nursery school became the center of the effort to save as many young children as possible.

Fred recalled a night when more than two dozen women were scheduled to be deported along with their children. The loading would be supervised personally by a top SS official, making escape difficult.

"Walter Süskind had alerted as many of us as possible to assist the mothers in carrying their babies past the SS guards," he said. "Each woman was provided with blankets which they carried in their arms after folding them a certain way, and in this fashion the transport took place."

As the women filed past the guards with their "blanket babies," each was counted as two people. In this way, the SS guards ended up with the correct total of people scheduled for deportation. As for the actual children, they'd been snuck out and brought to the nursery school. "From there they were placed with non-Jewish families until after the war, when it was

Young Jewish children sit at tables in the childcare center near the Hollandsche Schouwburg [theater used as deportation center] in the Amsterdam Jewish quarter in 1942. Staff of the childcare center and the college that housed it worked with the Jewish Council and Dutch underground to save children from being deported.

hoped to reunite them with their parents," said Fred. "Unfortunately that hope was realized only in a few very isolated cases."

This rescue effort was made possible thanks to the help of people at the nursery school and the college, working with the Jewish Council and the Dutch underground. Henriëtte Henriquez Pimentel, a member of a prominent Jewish Portuguese family in Amsterdam, headed the school. Along with Walter Süskind and Johan van Hulst, director of the teaching college, she helped save the lives of more than six hundred Jewish children.

The rescue operation lasted until July of 1943, when Nazis stormed the school, capturing both children and caretakers. Henriëtte Henriquez Pimentel was deported and murdered in a death camp. In 1944, Walter Süskind and his wife and daughter were arrested. His wife and daughter were murdered upon arriving at Auschwitz in October of 1944. Walter was killed on a death march from the camp in February of 1945. Johan van Hulst survived the war and passed away in 2018 at the age of 107.

I HAD TO ACT FAST

On June 20, 1943, Fred was just sitting down to breakfast with his mother and brother when they heard a loudspeaker from the street. The message blared that

Young Dutch Jewish children brought from the nursery to a children's home by the Dutch underground. The photo was taken sometime between 1941 and 1943.

Jews must turn themselves in to the police. This was a surprise *razzia*, or raid.

Fred and his family rushed outside. Spotting a Nazi patrol on the next corner, they headed the other way, and managed to reach the office of the Jewish Council without being caught.

Chaos reigned. Historian Jacob Presser has pointed out that at least one German official later boasted about how preparations for the June 20 "offensive" had been kept remarkably secret. The Jewish community was taken by surprise; no leaks gave any advance warning of the raid.

"I had to find a safe place for Hans and my mother,"

said Fred. "In one of the offices I detected a small door in the ceiling. I had to act fast—we moved a table right underneath that door and put a chair on top of it. Hans was now able to lift himself through the narrow opening in the ceiling." Hans disappeared inside the enclosed space and closed the little door behind him.

Fred's mother was carrying a small suitcase and a shopping bag. Confronted by an SS guard, she pleaded with him to let her go into a small room to rearrange her luggage. Fred, who was wearing a Jewish Council armband, slipped outside to help others. When an SS officer called off the name Angress as a Jewish Council employee exempt from deportation, his mother stepped forward to be counted. Fred, Hans, and his mother had escaped.

That was the only comfort Fred had on this terrifying day. That evening, Fred went to the train station, where his friends and neighbors were being loaded into cattle cars.

"The scene was indescribable. There was absolute silence as young and old were driven up the ramps; only an occasional whimpering could be heard as here and there a baby was carried by its parents into the dark, smelling cattle cars," he said.

"I spotted one of our neighbors, a young couple with their four-year-old daughter being pushed up the ramp by the SS. There was absolutely nothing I could do to help them—no way to even get the little girl out. I felt very helpless and desolate."

At nine o'clock, the long train pulled out in the darkness. "I would never forget the scene at the train station," said Fred.

Fred realized time was running out for him, for everyone. "There would be no more opportunities to help others. If I wanted to stay alive, I had to fight for survival. Those of us that were still 'exempt' did not know from one hour to the next how long our IDs would stay in effect."

Fred had already received a warning from an unlikely source. One of the most feared and ruthless SS commanders had entered Fred's office, closed the door behind him, and in a whisper confided that the war was not going in Germany's favor. His next words surprised everyone.

"If he were in our shoes, he would go into hiding as soon as possible. We didn't say a word, just nodded our heads," said Fred. "After he left we just looked at each other in disbelief. We could not believe the transformation of this man."

THE LAST RAID

Deportation of Jews had begun in the summer of 1942, and by the following summer, almost all Dutch Jews who hadn't gone into hiding were deported. The last raid took place on September 29, 1943; the Nazis then disbanded the Jewish Council. Professor Presser noted, "the total liquidation of Dutch Jewry was about to be consummated."

Fred had been warned just the day before. He passed on the information to everyone he saw, including a fellow worker named Abraham Pach. "'Abraham, this is it!'" Fred recalled telling him. "'Tonight everybody will be picked up. If you want to stay alive you have to go into hiding.'"

Fred felt anxious about his friend. "Going into hiding cost money and I knew that his family was in dire financial straits and it was not likely that he could hold out through the remainder of the war."

Fred feared he'd never see Abraham again. But to his amazement, after the war ended he ran into Abraham on the street one day. Fred assumed Abraham had miraculously survived a Nazi death camp and asked where he'd been sent. Fred recalled, "With a big smile on his face, his eyes sparkling, he replied that he had never been caught. 'I was in hiding with my wife—that's what YOU told me to do!'"

Although hiding seemed to offer the best chance of

survival, the truth was that not everyone could do it. Some people didn't have non-Jewish friends willing to help or enough money to buy food or pay for forged identity papers and food coupons. Others feared their punishment would be worse if they were caught hiding. Many who went on transports did not realize the truth: The Nazis were carrying out mass murder on a systematic, unimaginable scale.

GOING UNDER

On the day Fred received the last warning, he bicycled home to tell his mother and Hans. That very night, a friend took them in while they continued to make long-term arrangements. It wasn't possible for the three to hide together. Most non-Jewish families simply didn't have enough room or capacity to handle more than one or two people in hiding.

For the next nineteen months, a former neighbor Fred referred to only as Nolte became the family's contact with the outside world, helping to coordinate their needs and hiding places. The Angress family was lucky. They had sold their business, and the new owner was making monthly payments. Nolte collected this sum regularly and dispersed it to help pay for food for Fred, Hans, and their mother.

"'Going under' involved more than physically moving to another address," Fred explained. "It meant getting a new personality. We removed our yellow stars from all our clothing. The underground supplied us with new identification cards without the 'J' required by the Germans. These new IDs looked absolutely authentic, showing our new name and new places of residence."

From this point on, Fred would be known as Frits Mulder. "They also got food stamps for us, which were vital to our survival as food was scarce and the Dutch citizens had barely enough stamps to feed their own families. For the next nineteen months I stayed hidden, always facing the very real possibility of being denounced, knowing that the slightest slip would endanger not only my life, but the lives of the family that was harboring me."

For the first six months, Fred changed his "home" at least twelve times, while his friend Nolte searched for a safe, more permanent hiding situation. Sometimes Fred removed a door from its hinges to use it as a bed with a thin mattress. One family was very poor. "We ate onions for lunch, onions for dinner—lots of them; onion stew, onion soup. But I had no problem with that—it certainly beat getting arrested."

Once, Fred had a close call when three men in uniform arrived at the house where he was staying on the outskirts of Amsterdam. Fred was unable to hide in time. The men threatened to arrest him and asked a lot of questions. And then one demanded to know what it might be worth to Fred *not* to be turned in.

Suddenly, Fred realized what was happening. The men were blackmailers pretending to be Nazis! Fred handed over his watch and some money as a bribe to keep them quiet. He left that hiding situation for a new one as soon as he could.

NELLY AND HER FAMILY

Finally, Fred's luck—and life—changed for the better. "On March 24, 1944, I received the welcome news that the underground had found a permanent shelter for me. No longer would I need to move from place to place—a young couple with a three year old son was willing to take me in for the duration of the war."

Fred's protectors were Nelly and Gerard Bom, who had a young son named Maarten. "From the moment I entered their home, I became part of their family. I slept on a couch in their dining room. Gerard was able to obtain food stamps for me through his work with the underground.

"The days in hiding were long. The end of the war was as yet not in sight, and I did not dare to leave the apartment at any time. I tried to help Nelly as much as I could, keeping the house clean, doing the dishes." said Fred. The best part was babysitting little Maarten, whom he adored, and chatting each evening with Nelly and Gerard.

Like Fred, others in hiding remembered long, lonely days and the ever-present fear of being discovered. Burt Kaufmann, another young man who hid in Amsterdam, recalled one night as people gathered to listen to the BBC on the radio. At the time, there were more than ten people in the room, at least five in hiding. It was, of course, forbidden to have a radio set or to listen to British news programs, which reported on the Allies' progress in the war.

And so when Burt and the others suddenly heard a bell jingling on the gate outside, they sprang into action, certain they'd been found out. "The Jews went quickly to their hiding places . . . the radio set disappeared and then the husband went to open the gate," Burt said.

It turned out to be a false alarm. The neighbor's cat had jangled the bell—and everyone's nerves. It wasn't the only time Burt was forced to disappear quickly. Whenever he had to scramble for cover, he was careful to take along any object that might give him away. Even one chair left askew, or an extra glass or plate on the table, could arouse suspicion.

Nothing could be left to chance or the sharp eyes of the Nazis. Nazi sympathizers and informers, or blackmailers such as those Fred had met, were everywhere.

Burt's fiancée, Lissy Cohn, lived with a couple who sometimes sheltered up to six people. This required extra caution—even with the garbage. Burt explained, "Sometimes it was a problem to get rid of the potato peels, as the quantity was too big in proportion to the known number of persons of the household."

A group of Dutch resistance members and hidden Jews crowd into a room, most probably to listen to the news on a clandestine radio. The photo was taken sometime between November 1943 and May 1945.

THE HUNGER WINTER

The winter of 1944–1945 in the Netherlands became known as *Hongerwinter*, the Hunger Winter. The Germans blockaded fuel and supplies, causing widespread food shortages and famine. Although news that the Allies had invaded Normandy, France, on D-Day, June 6, 1944, raised Fred's spirits, the end of the war was still months away.

Because of the food shortage, Nelly moved with her husband and son to the countryside for a few months to stay with her sister. There wasn't room for Fred, so instead he was hidden by Nelly's mother, known as Mama Fey. Mama Fey worked in a drugstore pharmacy below her apartment. Fred lived upstairs in the attic. The days were long and the house freezing. Fred didn't dare go near the windows for fear of being seen. At night he listened to soldiers marching by, praying that no boots would stop outside the door.

Nelly's sister provided Fred and Mama Fey with crops from the previous harvest. Fred had begun his ordeal in hiding on a diet of onions, and now he ate beans all the time: green beans, yellow beans, and brown beans. In later life, Fred could never eat beans.

During this desperate time, the two daughters of the family hiding Burt Kaufmann decided to bicycle in winter to relatives' farms in the countryside to fetch produce for everyone. They never abandoned their commitment to Burt. "A few days before Christmas 1944, in ice and snow, they made a trip of 160 kilometers [about a hundred miles] by bicycle to a rural district."

And so Burt and the family hiding him subsisted on sugar beets—and even tulip bulbs. By this time, there was only a little wood or coal for fuel, and paraffin candles for light. There was no electricity. "Most people had nothing to lighten a room and went to bed at five o'clock in the afternoon."

Even in the most dire of circumstances, Fred and his protectors tried to not lose their humanity—and sense of humor. Fred was still freezing in Mama Fey's small attic room when Nelly's family returned from the countryside to celebrate little Maarten's birthday in December of 1944.

They didn't have much to eat, but to celebrate, Mama Fey concocted a homemade alcoholic drink from fruit and alcohol from the pharmacy. She'd been saving it for the end of the war. However, on this special occasion, she opened a bottle for the adults to try.

Fred was now twenty-one, but not at all used to alcohol. That powerful beverage went straight to his head. He locked himself in the bathroom and began to laugh so hysterically everyone came looking for him. When he finally was pushed upstairs to the attic and tumbled into bed, he dropped into a restful sleep, his first in a very long time. His antics gave everyone else a much-needed laugh.

Years later, Fred reflected that there were days when having a sense of humor was all that got them through. "And there were those times when we lost our courage and thought that we would never smile again."

FREEDOM

On May 8, 1945, the war in Europe was declared over. It had been almost five years to the date since the Germans had invaded the Netherlands. Fred had just turned twenty-two. Most of his teen years had been filled not with fun and parties with school friends, but with fear and the terror of seeing his community disintegrate.

Fred was excited to learn that his brother and mother were safe and had also made it through. Hans had been placed with Ton and Ali Kooy, a couple who had two sons of their own and treated Hans like a third. Hans later helped them immigrate to the United States.

But most astonishing was his mother's story. Mrs. Angress had decided not to hide. Instead, she lived openly in a boardinghouse that, unbelievably, also housed German officers. Her false papers identified her as Henny Kiefer (her actual maiden name), a victim from the bombed-out city of Rotterdam.

"Instead of keeping a low profile and staying indoors

in a neighborhood where she was well known, she walked around on the streets in broad daylight, keeping her weekly appointments at the beauty parlor to have her hair and nails done," said Fred.

Henny even made a point to greet the German officers warmly whenever she encountered them. They had no idea their attractive, stylish neighbor was a Jewish woman.

Fred's mother had also found a way to get extra money. The boardinghouse owner's brother was a member of the Dutch Nazi Party. He ran a shoe business and sometimes kept new stock in a closet near Henny's room. Somehow, Henny got herself a key and used it to help herself to a pair or two of shoes on occasion. She didn't dare wear them, of course, but she sold the shoes to a contact to buy extra food on the black market.

MOTHER'S DAY, 1945

On Mother's Day, 1945, Henny Kiefer Angress opened her door to find a handsome young American sergeant smiling at her. She hadn't seen her son Werner for more than five years, since he had escaped to America. Werner's story was also remarkable. He joined the United States Army at age eighteen. When the Allies invaded Normandy on D-Day, Werner was there, jumping behind Utah Beach as a paratrooper in the 82nd Airborne Division. After being wounded, Werner had briefly become a prisoner of war.

After his release, Werner served as an interrogator of German prisoners. In the spring of 1945, Werner was an interpreter for General James Gavin. That May, General Gavin granted the young soldier's unusual request: to "borrow" an official jeep and take a few days of leave to try to find his family in the Netherlands.

The spirited Henny Angress died in 1985, shortly before her ninety-third birthday. Werner was awarded the Bronze Star and Purple Heart. He attended Stanford University and became a distinguished professor. Werner returned to Germany, where he died in 2010. Both Fred and Hans also came to the United States.

In Fred's 1989 recollection of his wartime experiences, entitled "Survival in the Lions' Den," Fred wrote, "Forty-three years have passed since the end of WWII . . . but they are not enough to erase my memories. I still suffer from nightmares in which the Germans chase me. Just when they catch me, I wake up, drenched in sweat."

In 1973, Fred and his wife traveled to the Netherlands to visit Nelly. She had remarried after her first husband died and was now Nelly Gispen. After twenty-six years, Fred wondered if they'd even recognize each other. Fred emerged from the train. Suddenly, he heard someone shout his name. He ran to embrace his old friend. Those twenty-six years had disappeared.

In January of 1982, in a ceremony in Amsterdam, Nelly Gispen received the Yad Vashem award recognizing her as one of the Righteous Among the Nations, an international program at the Yad Vashem world Holocaust remembrance center in Israel that honors non-Jews who took risks to save Jewish people during the Holocaust.

When Nelly wrote to tell Fred about the speeches, she said, "'One of the speakers said exactly what I told you at the time, 'We are no heroes, but things just came our way.'"

To Fred Angress and his family, Nelly would always be a hero.

In 1989, when Fred Angress sent a copy of his memoir to the archives of the Leo Baeck Institute, he dedicated it to Nelly Gispen. Here's what he wrote:

"To Nelly Gispen, my dear friend, who with her courage and love has seen me safely through a time of evil and destruction.

She gave me shelter, when I had no place to go.

She gave me encouragement, when I had no hope.

She could make me laugh when I was sad.

She would listen when I needed to talk.

She did so by endangering her own life and the safety of her family.

I will never forget her."

CHILDREN IN HIDING

Fred Angress was twenty when he went into hiding; he understood the danger and the obstacles he faced. Many Jewish parents had to make the heart-wrenching decision to entrust neighbors or strangers with babies and small children too young to understand what was happening. These parents couldn't know if their children would be safe or if they'd ever see them again.

Left: Alfred Münzer (on the tricycle) was born on November 23, 1941, in The Hague, a city in the Netherlands. In 1942, when Alfred was still a baby, his parents put him into the care of neighbors to be hidden. His first home was too dangerous, so he was placed with Dutch Indonesian rescuer Tolé Madna and his family until his mother was able to claim him after the war. Even after Alfred and his mother immigrated to the United States, he remained close to the Madna family.

Right: Alfred Münzer and Tolé Madna, who hid him, sit outside holding chickens during a postwar visit in 1946 or 1947. Alfred, now an American physician, always called Mr. Madna "Papa," and was able to go to the Netherlands to say goodbye before his beloved rescuer died at age ninety-six.

Photographs of Rita in her different hiding-homes with her different hiding mothers, fathers and sisters/brothers during 1942-44.

Many children in hiding lived with more than one family during the war. Rita Serphos was born in the Netherlands in 1939. Her mother, Miep, who was blond and blue-eyed, passed as a Christian and joined the resistance. She dyed Rita's hair blond, and moved her to a new situation every few months as a precaution against capture. She also taught Rita to call each new rescuer Papa and Mama. This photo album page shows the different places Rita was hidden in the Netherlands between 1942 and 1944.

Chapter Four
CHELLA: TRY AND BE BRAVE

AGAINST ALL ODDS, TWO SISTERS SURVIVE

*We are going to carry you over
these mountains no matter what.*

Rachella (Chella) Velt was born on May 15, 1928, in The Hague, the Netherlands. Chella's sister, Flora, was a few years older and was born on December 20, 1924.

Like Anne and Margot Frank, with whom they were fairly close in age (Anne was born a year after Chella, in 1929; Margot in 1926), the Velt sisters were captured after an informer betrayed their family's hiding place. But while Anne and Margot both died of typhus at Bergen-Belsen concentration camp in 1945, Chella and

Flora survived, enduring more than a year and a half of hard labor, forced marches, and horrific ordeals in Nazi camps, including Auschwitz. The war ended just days before Chella turned seventeen.

Some people might have kept silent, trying to forget the devastating heartbreak and suffering. Yet for more than twenty-five years, Chella Velt shared her experiences with thousands of young people and adults.

"I lost so much that was dear to me, and I've experienced so much pain, that I feel the stories should be told," Chella said in an interview with the Oregon Jewish Museum and Center for Holocaust Education (OJMCHE) in Portland, where she lived for many years. "It was people that did it. And I would like people to know that regular people like them let it happen."

Chella went on to say she felt that "young people have a duty to not sit back and be bystanders, but be active in government and realize what goes on."

When Chella was five, her mother died. Her father, Israel Velt, had a job that required travel, which made it difficult for him to care for two young daughters on his own. So he placed Chella and Flora in a Jewish orphanage for about four years. This experience brought the

Rachella (Chella) Velt in 1936 when she was about eight. She is holding a *schultüte*, or school cone, filled with small toys and sweets and traditionally given to children on the first day of school.

sisters close. They were able to return home in January of 1940 after their father's remarriage.

Chella turned twelve in May of 1940, just as German soldiers stormed into the Netherlands. "Because Holland is a very small distance from Germany, [they] just walked in. In an hour they were walking through the streets; they were everywhere in Holland," Chella said. "The boots and the noise. Just as you can imagine it, that's the way it sounded. We stood on the side of the street watching them come in."

At the start of the Nazi occupation, life for Jewish

families continued much the same. By 1942, Chella noticed an increase in antisemitism. She'd gotten a new bicycle: It was her prized possession. It broke her heart when the Nazis issued a rule requiring all Jews to turn in their bicycles.

When Chella was forced to wear the Star of David badge, some of her non-Jewish neighbors were sympathetic. A few even sewed stars on their own clothes in solidarity. But outright resistance carried a price. "People, if they spoke up, would get arrested, and they would be interrogated," Chella said.

On February 25, 1941, Dutch workers organized a

Rachella and Flora Velt in the 1930s.

strike to protest the arrest of several hundred young Jews. The Nazis suppressed this defiance and began to escalate their persecution of the Jewish population. That meant that most resistance efforts took place in secret. The Dutch underground was a grassroots resistance movement that involved forging false identity documents, producing underground publications, and helping Jewish families to go into hiding.

THE STRANGER AT THE DOOR

One day, Chella's sister received a letter with instructions to report to the police station in two weeks for an assignment in a work camp. (When Anne Frank's older sister, Margot, received a similar letter in July of 1942, the entire Frank family went into hiding.)

Flora's letter warned that if she didn't comply, her family would suffer consequences. Chella dissolved into tears. "I went berserk," said Chella. "I said, 'Don't let Flora go! Don't let Flora go!'"

In the midst of their panic, the doorbell rang. Chella's father opened it to find a stranger standing there. "'I'm from the Dutch underground, and I know you have a young girl in your house,'" he told Mr. Velt. "'Now give us your child, and we will see to it. We will hide her.'"

Was he an informer or could he be trusted? Chella's

family had no way of knowing. The man said he'd return in a week and urged them to think it over.

"We didn't sleep that night. I crept into bed with Flora and we trembled all night long," said Chella. "My father stayed up all hours of the night."

Meanwhile, they followed the letter's instructions. They prepared a suitcase for Flora and told all their neighbors and friends Flora would comply with the order. Secrecy was essential. Then one day soon after, Chella returned home from school to find her sister gone. To protect Chella in case she was questioned, her father and stepmother wouldn't tell her where Flora was.

Yet Chella couldn't rest until she knew if Flora had gone to the labor camp or not. At last her parents relented. Her sister, for the moment at least, was safe. Flora had disappeared into hiding.

THE SECOND LETTER

Chella's father and his brothers-in-law got letters next. Chella remembered her uncles coming to the house to discuss what to do. She listened as the men sat around the dining room table, drinking tea and weighing their options.

It wasn't easy to arrange hiding; her father and his relatives all feared putting their families at risk. They tried to assure themselves things wouldn't get too bad. The Netherlands was, after all, their home. Jews had been living peacefully here for years. Even under Nazi occupation, surely the remaining Dutch officials wouldn't let anything happen to them.

Not long after, Chella came home from school to find only her stepmother: Her father was gone. Unwilling to risk repercussions for his family or any scrutiny about Flora's whereabouts, Chella's father had decided to obey the letter.

YOUR HEART STOPPED IN YOUR THROAT

Chella was now attending a Jewish school. Each week there were fewer students in class. Some were hauled out of their homes; others, like Flora, had gone into hiding. Sometimes, Chella spotted military trucks parked outside the building. One friend was snatched right out of the classroom. "Your heart stopped in your throat because you thought they were coming for you," Chella said.

One day Chella came home from school to an empty house. Frightened, she sat alone, not knowing what to think. What had happened to her stepmother? At last, to Chella's relief, her aunt arrived. She explained that Chella's stepmother had gone to stay in a hospital for a while to stay safe. Sometimes doctors and nurses provided temporary protection for Jews at risk for deportation until more permanent hiding places could be found.

Chella wouldn't be living at home anymore either. The time had come for them all to go into hiding. Her aunt told her to pack a bag with a nightgown and some clean clothes. Chella should use her schoolbag only: It mustn't look as if she were going on a long trip.

Her aunt waited with Chella until dark. Then a local shopkeeper who was part of the Dutch underground arrived. Chella walked with him to his store, not knowing what to expect. To Chella's astonishment, her sister was there. Flora had been hiding in a back room of his shop for months!

"'What will happen now, Flora?'" Chella remembered asking.

Her sister replied, "'Who knows? We are together now, so let's see what happens. At least we are together.'"

For the next six or seven months, Chella and Flora lived in the rear of the shop. Eventually, Chella's stepmother and her father, who'd managed to get out of the labor camp after a bad accident, joined them. Once, during a surprise search, they all had to rush upstairs. They barely made it: Chella's father had broken his legs and had trouble walking.

The four squeezed into a space behind a clothes

closet. There they waited, not daring to move. Chella was terrified. "If someone had coughed or sneezed or anything—it was so quiet . . . and such a terrible, frightening experience."

Hiding four people was very difficult. The Velt family couldn't stay together for long. The shopkeeper and his family moved to a smaller house with only one small attic room. So members of the Dutch underground helped Flora find a new hiding place, posing as a live-in maid in Rotterdam; Chella was sent to live with a family that had five children.

Chella liked her new protectors, even though she had to stay inside almost all the time. In the evenings, she tried to study alongside the other children. All went well until the day an unexpected house-to-house search took place.

Frantically, Chella locked herself in the bathroom. She could hear boots stomping loudly, entering one room, then the next. Then the sound stopped right outside the bathroom. A man demanded, "'Open the door!'"

Without missing a beat, the mother of the family called out, "'Oh, my little girl is sick. She has a terrible stomach ache. She has been on the toilet all day long today.'"

The man gave up and left. Chella was safe, but so shaken up she dissolved in tears. It had been a close call.

THE BIRTHDAY VISIT

Sometimes, on dark nights, the children of the family took Chella around the block, just so she could breathe the fresh air. That was risky enough. In early 1944, when Chella had been in hiding for more than a year, she did something far more dangerous.

Chella missed her father so much she decided to visit him on his birthday. He hadn't been well since his accident in the labor camp and needed a walking stick to get around. Chella got word to Flora; both girls arrived safely at the house where their parents were in hiding. It was a wonderful visit, and they stayed together in the tiny attic room for a week.

But when a member of the Dutch underground came to deliver food ration cards, she issued a warning to the sisters. "'It was very foolish what you did,'" she told Chella and Flora. "'You shouldn't go out in the street. . . . They [the Nazis] stop people. They interrogate. Be careful. Go home and stay where you are.'"

Chella didn't want to leave her own family. Besides, everything seemed fine. They enjoyed long hours reading and making plans for what they would do when the war ended. Then came the morning when Chella was awakened by strange voices in the house. "'We've come to get the family Velt. Where are they? There are four of them.'"

Minutes later, the door burst open and two big Dutch policemen with guns barged in.

Chella had often had nightmares about being arrested. Now she sat up in bed and cried, "'It's my dream. It's my dream. It's not true.'"

"'It is true, Chella,'" her father said. "'Do as they tell you, but be brave.'"

Chella later discovered someone had informed on them. The Velts were marched to the police station; the shopkeeper hiding them was arrested.

The Velt family's capture, like that of the Frank family, wasn't unusual. Historians estimate that between 25,000 and 35,000 people went into hiding in the Netherlands. About two-thirds of those avoided capture and survived.

Of the approximately 107,000 Jews who were deported from the Netherlands and sent to camps, only 5,200 survived. There were about 150,000 Jews living in the Netherlands in 1940, including about 25,000 German Jews who, like Fred Angress and his family, had come as refugees. In the postwar census of 1947, only about 15,000 Jews were counted.

I'M NOT LETTING GO

At the police station, Chella was separated from her father. Even at fifteen, Chella was determined to protect the other family with five children who'd been hiding her for months. She didn't think the police knew their address.

So she didn't mention them at all, claiming that she'd only been at the home where she'd been caught. "I felt all the time I must not say that I had stayed with that family with five kids. I must save them."

From the station, the girls and their stepmother were brought to a jail. As they were being escorted, the policeman told Chella he'd walked their father on the same route earlier in the day. Mr. Velt had made an impression on the man, and he recounted their father's words to his daughters.

As he limped painfully along, Chella's father had pointed up at the tram cables overhead, telling the policeman, "'My life hangs on that cable, and it can snap any time, but as long as the tram hangs onto that cable, I will hang onto that line and I will fight with all my might . . . And I hope my family will do the same because willingly I'm not going to let go of that cable.'"

The sisters and their stepmother were put into a cell in a women's area of the jail. Some of the inmates were Jewish prisoners, while others were members of the Dutch underground.

"In the other cell was a girl who had worked for the underground who would sing at night. She had a

Prisoners boarding a deportation train in the Westerbork transit camp in 1943 or 1944. On July 14, 1942, a systematic transfer of all Jews from the Netherlands to Westerbork began. Deportations from Westerbork to killing centers in Poland began the next day. An estimated 102,000 Jews and a few hundred Roma passed through Westerbork.

beautiful voice and she would sing . . . songs of freedom. She was in isolation, that girl. She would scream out," said Chella. "They would punish her . . . but she would not give in. Her spirit was such an example to all of us. There were people like that who would not bend under the power or the rule of the Germans. She was a fantastic girl."

Two women gave Chella advice. "'Look, there is only one thing to do. We play some cards, we read books, and we keep our sanity. We don't cry. We try and be brave and see the day through.'"

Books were passed from cell to cell. Chella devoured books from morning to night. "That saved me."

A few weeks later, Chella and her family were put on a train to Westerbork, a camp near the Dutch border with Germany. The Nazis were now using Westerbork as a transit camp for Jews who were kept there for only a short time before being deported east to Nazi death camps in Poland.

While there were escape attempts, most failed. "People asked me afterwards how come you didn't fight back. . . . But it is very hard to look down a barrel [of a gun] and have strong men stand around you with guns and to try to make a run for it," said Chella.

Chella and Flora got lucky at Westerbork. They met

an old friend named John who had a job at the camp. He offered to put their names on a list for people to go to another camp in the Netherlands called Vught, also known as Herzogenbusch. It would, at least temporarily, keep them from being sent to Auschwitz or another death camp in Poland. Chella, who was still only fifteen, hesitated. She didn't want to leave her father.

Because of his past injury, Chella's dad was in the sickbed section of the camp and Chella was able to visit him. When she told him about the chance to go to Vught, he urged her and Flora to grab it.

Chella's father tried to reassure her they'd meet again. "'You come and find me after the war. I will be there waiting for you to find me,'" Mr. Velt told Chella. "'I will keep myself fit and strong, and I will fight with all my might. That is what I want you to do. Stay here [at Vught in the Netherlands] with your sister.'"

YOU CAN DO ANYTHING

Chella and Flora got on the list to be transferred to Vught. A week later, it was time for them to go. Chella had to say her last goodbye to her father. To reassure her, Israel Velt threw down his walking stick to prove he could still walk unaided and was strong enough to survive.

He declared, "'Anything you want to do in life, if you put your mind to it, you can do that, Chella. I want

View of the barbed wire fence and a watchtower at Vught in the Netherlands after the liberation of the camp in October of 1944. Chella and her sister were sent to this camp from Westerbork.

you to remember that. . . . So you be sure that you do anything that you have to do.'"

Chella hugged him and ran out. She didn't dare look back.

The next morning, she and Flora left on a train for Vught. Much later, Chella learned that while her step-mother survived, her father was gassed on arrival at Auschwitz.

Records show that Israel Salomon Velt was mur-dered at Auschwitz on March 26, 1944, at the age of fifty-four. Chella never forgot his parting words. His strength and love sustained her for her entire life.

In Westerbork, Chella and Flora had been allowed to wear their own clothes. At Vught, they were given striped prison uniforms. At first, the sisters were assigned to a work detail in the Philips factory that was part of the camp.

Frederik Jacques Philips, who died in 2005 at the age of one hundred, was the head of his family's elec-tronics firm. Philips has received both praise and condemnation for his actions during World War II. On the one hand, his company contributed to the German war effort. On the other, he has been cred-ited with hiring many Jews and trying to keep them from being sent to Auschwitz by telling the Nazis the workers couldn't be replaced. For her part, Chella felt being a member of the Philips group of Dutch workers saved her life.

At the outset, it appeared that working at Philips might even protect Chella and Flora from being deported out of the Netherlands. One night at Vught, the sisters were woken up. They were ordered to line up and march to a train outside the gate. Just as they were about to board, they were sent back to the barracks. Word spread throughout the camp: Mr. Philips had helped them gain a reprieve from deportation.

"Mr. Philips had flown to Germany and had told the German officials he would keep the people there and he would produce more," Chella said. "He had really saved our lives again. We were sent back to the barracks and we went to work again the next day. We thought, 'We were really saved this time. Maybe we will never be sent away.'"

Chella's hopes were short-lived. Like all Dutch Jews, the Philips workers couldn't escape the Nazis' relentless system of deportation and extermination. Holocaust historian Nikolaus Wachsmann has noted, "The truth about Nazi intentions was slowly dawning on them [the Philips group], but their special status in the camp could not save them from deportation, and in early June 1944, the SS removed the last group of Jews from Herzogenbusch [Vught]."

Chella celebrated her sixteenth birthday at Vught on May 15. About two weeks later, she and the other Philips workers were again called to the trains.

This time, there was no reprieve.

AUSCHWITZ

"We were in those cattle wagons for four days and four nights," said Chella. "We traveled through Germany, and when we passed through the border from Germany, we threw little bits of papers with our names on them through the slats of the cattle wagons."

Chella had heard that railway workers had been known to pick up the papers and send them to the names of friends written on the front. "Many, of course, were trampled . . . and were never found."

They were given no food on the train. As they rumbled along, the landscape changed, becoming dark and forested. They stopped at a station and were taken into a camp. This was Auschwitz.

Almost immediately, Chella, one of the youngest there, fell desperately sick with dysentery, a severe intestinal disorder. She lost weight and could barely swallow the dry bread Flora urged her to nibble. Flora wouldn't let her give up. "One day I wouldn't eat, and Flora smacked me. 'You eat,' she said. 'You eat if you choke on it. You are going to eat and swallow that food.'"

It was a brutal place. Chella was ordered to stand at attention, sometimes naked, for hours. No matter what, she and Flora stuck together, holding hands so they wouldn't be split up. Once, when they ended up in separate lines, Chella slipped over to join her sister, panicked at being apart. "I thought, 'If we go, we go together.'"

CHOICELESS CHOICES

The sisters were put to work carrying and moving bricks at the Auschwitz gates, where they could see trainloads of exhausted prisoners arrive. Chella soon learned most people were taken down a road that led to gas chambers. "Many, many years after I can still see that road . . . I couldn't stand it anymore, the agony and the pain."

Chella also realized that having workers at the gates where the new arrivals could see them was done, in part, to prevent panic. This was, very likely, part of the hideous deception efforts by SS guards. They told prisoners they were headed to the baths, hiding the truth of what awaited. When they could, Auschwitz inmates tried to warn newcomers about the selection process that sent some people to immediate death.

"Some new arrivals learned the truth just in time," Professor Wachsmann notes. "As they climbed off the trains, inmates from the Canada Commando [or

Kanada Kommando, a work group of inmates who later took victims' possessions and clothing to a warehouse called Kanada, so named because Canada was a country associated with wealth] defied SS orders and told them three basic rules for the selections: Act strong and healthy, claim to be between sixteen and forty years old, hand young children to elderly relatives. . . .

"Mothers, in particular, faced a split-second decision," Wachsmann continues. "To abandon their children on the barely comprehensible advice of a stranger? Or to join them and stand with a group ominously made up of the elderly and frail? There was no right decision based on ordinary moral norms."

It was, rather, what Holocaust scholar Lawrence Langer has called one of the "'choiceless choices'" of Auschwitz.

LET ME CARRY IT

Weak, feverish, and in constant pain, sixteen-year-old Chella began to give up hope and long for death. She cried out, asking God to take her. "I really prayed to die, but Flora heard me, she came to me, and she took my bricks off my arms. She said, 'Let me carry it, Chella.'"

Flora took two of Chella's four bricks. Spying this, a female guard whipped Flora and made her carry five or six bricks at a time for the rest of the day. Chella said, "There was no pity."

Chella got through that day, and the one after it. And then she made it through the week. Their next job was cutting up bricks to make a road. They were forced to work from early morning until late, and Chella wasn't sure how much longer she could hang on. "We were going insane with the agony around us. It was very hard to live. Just to survive each day was a miracle."

Then one day their group was called together. A man from the Telefunken electronics factory had come to interview them about the factory work they'd done in Vught. It seemed Mr. Philips had reported that the Dutch workers were highly trained and therefore valuable to the war effort. Several weeks later, the Dutch group was ordered to get ready.

"We were there [in Auschwitz] about six weeks, a couple of months, and I thought if we had to stay there another week or two, half of us would die," Chella said. "There we were, and we were being marched out of the gate of Auschwitz."

As she walked out, Chella prayed with all her heart. "'God, if you are listening keep us safe and save these people out of this hell. Save them.'"

Most were not saved. Located in Nazi-occupied Poland, Auschwitz was the Nazis' largest camp complex, encompassing three camps and Birkenau, or Auschwitz II, a killing center with gas chambers. The

USHMM estimates that approximately 1.3 million people, including Jews, Roma people, Soviet prisoners of war, and non-Jewish Poles, among others, were deported to the complex between 1940 and 1945, when it was liberated by the Soviet army. More than 1.1 million people were murdered there; nearly one million of these innocent victims were Jews.

In 1947, a memorial and museum were established at Auschwitz. Today it also serves as a center for international education and research about the Holocaust and genocide.

Chella, Flora, and other women in the Philips group were taken by train to Reichenbach, in eastern Germany, not far from the border with Czechoslovakia. There, they lived in a small camp and worked at a Telefunken factory, which made use of Jewish slave labor as well as regular German workers.

"It was the same type of work that we had done for Philips," Chella said. "Indeed, he really had secured our lives, this man [Mr. Philips]. . . . We were treated as workers during the day there." Chella and the others had eight-hour shifts and also received a hot meal.

While conditions were better, there were constant reminders of how fragile their lives were under Hitler.

At the end of each workday, the women were marched from the Telefunken factory back to the camp.

"I remember the little children on the side of the road, and as we would walk to the camp they would spit on us, little kids five years of age," said Chella. "They were taught that those were *Juden* [Jews], and they would make remarks and all that. I couldn't believe it, how they had burned hate into little children that age."

NOT ENOUGH PEOPLE SPOKE UP

Although the German workers at the factory weren't supposed to interact with or even talk to the Jewish prisoners, one young woman named Lila Sommerfeld tried to show her compassion. She placed some bread and meat in the bottom drawer of the worktable, so Chella and the others could sneak bites of extra food. It didn't last long: Lila was seen, interrogated, and accused of collaborating. Yet her action mattered to Chella.

"She made such a big impression on me," said Chella. "She did show that there must have been one or two who did maybe care, but they were so far and few between . . . that's why all these things happened . . . because there was not enough people who spoke up. They were afraid. They were very much afraid."

Telefunken factories made radio transmitters and

devices involved in air raid defense; Chella recalled working on some sort of lamps. Even as Chella and the other Dutch prisoners were urged to go faster, they tried to slow down. Their sabotage had a dual purpose: It disrupted production for the German war effort, but it also kept them working—and alive.

"We didn't really want to help them. But we had to do it, and if we didn't do it somebody else would do it. We were saving our lives with it. We were put to work at it, but we tried to do [it] as slow as we could," Chella explained.

YOU ARE BEAUTIFUL

At the end of one workday, a Jewish worker in Chella's group dropped an entire tray of lamps. When she returned to the camp that night, she was beaten for this act of sabotage. As punishment, the others in her unit, including Flora, had their heads shaved.

When Flora returned to the barracks, Chella tried to make her sister feel better, saying, "'Oh, you are so fortunate to have such a beautiful head.'" All that night, as they cried together, Chella told her big sister, "'You are beautiful, Flora. Look how beautiful you are. You are much better looking than the other girls with the bald heads.'"

By the winter of 1945, the tide of war had turned in favor of the Allies. Allied bombers kept up their air assault on German cities; the Russian front was advancing and driving the German army back. One day, sirens in the factory began to blare.

During the bombing raid, Chella and the others hid in a field and cheered. She never felt afraid of the bombs. Instead, she welcomed the raids because "we really wanted everything destroyed for them."

Soon after, the factory was closed and the workers evacuated. Chella and her group were told they'd be going on a long walk. They were led toward Czechoslovakia on what was, in effect, a death march along icy roads and over snow-covered mountains.

This time, it was Chella who kept her sister alive. Flora had contracted pneumonia and was also suffering from blinding headaches. In one camp, Flora was put in the sick barracks, but Chella managed to get in and haul her out. She knew anyone too sick to walk or work would be killed.

"I made her get out of there, took her back into the barracks where we were. She went to work the next day," said Chella. "I thought, this was my turn, and I said to her, 'You have to get up.'"

Flora went on bravely, but she was sick, short of breath, and exhausted. Once, as they marched five in a row on a road, Flora ran over to the guard, begging, "'Shoot me. Shoot me, please. I want to be out of this life.'

"I was frightened to death that she did that," said Chella. "I ran after her. He [the guard] stopped everybody from walking, and he laughed at her and said, 'Look at this one with the bald head. She wants me to shoot her. Shall we shoot her?'"

Chella pleaded with the guard to ignore Flora and dragged her back in line. She slapped Flora's face to startle her, crying, "'You are going to walk. You are going to lean on me and on the girl next to you, and we are going to carry you over these mountains no matter what. You are going to walk and lean on us. You are not going to do that ever again.'

"She started to cry, and I said, 'Look, Flo, you just keep on walking and don't look behind you or anything. Don't go up to anybody anymore. Just walk.'"

THESE ARE FOR MY SISTER

Somehow, Chella never knew how, she had the strength to keep going, all the while helping Flora stagger forward step after painful step. The group now numbered about a hundred women. They tried to support one another. Sometimes they even sang, defying their captors' intentions to crush their spirits. Chella remembered everyone calling out, "'Let's sing songs. Let's show them.'" They sang the Dutch national anthem.

Chella was struggling too. She'd worn off the sole on one of her boots and had a huge blood blister on her foot. There was snow and gravel on the road. Flora walked up to a girl who had a pair of spare boots and simply took them from her, announcing, "'These are for my sister.'"

From a camp in Czechoslovakia the women were put in cattle trains, crammed in horrific conditions together with other prisoners from different places. Fights broke out and people became violent out of desperation. Chella convinced a friend who knew German to ask the guards to move all the Dutch women into one train car. Incredibly, the guards agreed.

The sense of community that had kept this group of women together for nearly a year now helped them to survive this new ordeal. Although the conditions were still desperate, they tolerated and cared for one another.

Chella said, "We all knew each other and none of us were going to hurt each other. That saved our lives again . . . I swear if we had gone back in the other cattle wagon none of us would have come out alive."

The trains took Chella, Flora, and the others to a salt

mine. Once again, they were put to hard labor. Food rations were meager; at one point Flora stole potato peels to make a sort of vegetable soup. To Chella, it tasted like the most delicious chicken soup ever. The sisters ate it all, including the peels.

The women had begun to hear rumors that the war was coming to an end. After several weeks in the salt mine, they were taken to a camp in Hanover, Germany. As the train passed by the city, Chella could see burned-out buildings, the results of heavy bombing by the Allies.

By now, many of the women were ill and severely malnourished. Chella couldn't help but wonder how long she and Flora and the rest could hold on.

YOU ARE FREE

"One day in the beginning of May, we got called on to stand to attention out in the yard, in front of the bar-racks. We were told that we were going to go on [a] transport," remembered Chella. "Well, every time you heard that word it was very, very frightening because you never knew what it meant."

Once again, they were herded onto a train. Some of the women feared this was the end. The train had to stop while the tracks were repaired. When it started up again, Chella sensed a change. She realized they were at the Danish border.

When they stopped, members of the Danish Red

Cross boarded the train. "They said to us in German, 'You are in Denmark now. You are free.' We said, 'Are you sure? Are you sure? Is it really true? It is not true. You are not telling us the truth.'

"We touched them and they said, 'It is true. You are in Denmark. We are going to take you to a town and to a camp where you are going to get a bath and you are going to have good food. You are free. The war is over. . . .'

"I remember sitting down in a corner, huddled and crying and crying and saying, 'Thank you, God, that you helped us. You did help us. Oh thank you, God. Thank you, God.' I kept on saying it over and over again. We kissed each other and we hugged each other. 'It is really true? We are really free? You mean we are not going to go to another camp? We're free!' It was just unbelievable."

The women were taken to Copenhagen; later they learned they were part of an effort spearheaded by Count Folke Bernadotte of Sweden to save prisoners at the end of the war. At the station in Copenhagen, Chella remembered one man in plain clothes who shook everyone's hand and welcomed them to Denmark.

Later, Chella discovered she had met King Christian X of Denmark.

From Denmark, the women were taken by boat to Sweden. During the crossing, the Red Cross representatives listened as Chella and the others told their stories.

Female Dutch Jewish survivors who were part of the "Philips" group go for a boat ride in Göteborg, Sweden, in 1945. Chella and Flora Velt were part of the group rescued through the efforts of Count Folke Bernadotte in the spring of 1945. Also in the group was Gitel (or Gisele) Münzer, whose son, Alfred, was hidden by an Indonesian Dutch family in the Netherlands. Photos of Alfred and his protectors can be seen elsewhere in this book.

To Chella's surprise, their listeners began to cry. Chella had noticed the same thing when they'd walked from the train in Copenhagen to the harbor: People lining the streets had tears streaming down their cheeks.

Later, after seeing newspaper photos, Chella understood why seeing the newly freed prisoners moved others to tears. "We were like walking skeletons . . . we were so worn and so filthy and thin, and bad looking, that the people kept on saying, 'Congratulations! Freedom! Freedom!' to us.

"It must have been a sight to behold. We were smiling, we were happy, and we were waving and throwing kisses to them. We were so happy. It was evidently a terrible sight for them to see, and they were very touched by it."

At the dock, a band played the Dutch national anthem. Hearing the music triggered something inside Chella.

"Well, that's when I started to cry, and I didn't stop crying for twenty-four hours," she said. "I was able to let go of it right away, of my emotions. I just cried and cried, but many people couldn't. I just cried and I don't remember when I stopped. The tears kept on flowing."

It was one week before her seventeenth birthday.

Chella, Flora, and the others were put in quarantine for six weeks to check for communicable diseases. They were also given baths and treated for lice, malnutrition, and other medical problems. Tests showed that Flora had developed tuberculosis, and she had to spend time in a sanatorium.

Their recovery took months. They learned that although their father had been murdered, their step-mother had survived and had gone to England to live with her three sisters. Eventually, Chella and Flora were able to visit England. While there, Chella met her first husband, Daniel Meekcoms.

Before getting married, though, Chella decided she wanted to live in the Netherlands for a year. She needed to walk the streets of her childhood and visit her old home. "I remember walking by the door and touching it and crying because so much had happened . . . We were so grateful to be alive, but the pain came back. The pain for what had gone . . .

"Why us? That question goes through your mind, from all those millions of people, how come we survived? Surely we were no better than anybody else. Surely we were no stronger than anybody else."

Chella believed that being part of the Philips group helped her and Flora survive. She felt fortunate that they hadn't been captured until late in the war, and she gave credit to those who'd hidden them for months.

"I'm very grateful to those Dutch people who did hide us. They were tremendous people who risked their lives. There was a tremendous underground in

Holland. I can't praise them enough for what they did. The first people I went to visit were the people I stayed with during the war [the family with five children]. It was fantastic seeing them again. I loved them."

Chella remained in contact with that family after marrying Daniel Meekcoms and immigrating to the United States in 1952. The couple settled in Portland, Oregon, where Flora had gone to live with her husband. Chella and Daniel had three children before divorcing. Chella went on to marry Holocaust survivor Jakob Kryszek in 1989. Chella and Jakob helped create the Oregon Holocaust Memorial in Washington Park in Portland, Oregon, in 2004.

DO YOU GIVE OF YOURSELF?

At the close of her 1976 interview, Chella reflected again on the words of her father. "He used to say to me, 'If you stand in front of the mirror and you look into the mirror, do you like what you see? Ask yourself that question. You have to live with that. Do you like what you see? Do you give of yourself what you really are?'"

Throughout her long life, Chella gave of herself through her courage in sharing her story, and in her work for tolerance and awareness. Chella's sister, Flora Velt Kirk, died in 1987. Chella passed away in 2013 at the age of eighty-five.

LOOK, LISTEN, REMEMBER: You can hear Chella's voice at the Oregon Jewish Museum and Center for Holocaust Education website: http://www.ojmche.org /oral-history-people/velt-chella.

PART TWO

Families
Torn Apart

True Stories from France

My childhood was not unusual for my time in history; what was unusual was my good fortune. One-and-a-half million children like me are not able to indulge in their memoirs today. . . .

Why was I saved when so many were not? I do not know the answer.

—RUTH OPPENHEIMER DAVID,
Holocaust survivor

The first German troops to return from the conquests of Poland and France march through the Brandenburg Gate in Berlin, July 18, 1940.

ABOUT THE PEOPLE IN PART TWO

RUTH OPPENHEIMER DAVID was born in Frankfurt, Germany, on March 17, 1929. She grew up in a small village with her parents and five siblings. In June of 1939, Ruth escaped to England through the rescue effort called the Kindertransport. Her three older siblings also left before World War II was declared on September 3, 1939. Her parents and two younger siblings were deported from Germany to Gurs internment camp in France. Rescuers were able to save her younger brother and sister, but Ruth's parents were deported and murdered at Auschwitz.

HANNE (JOHANNA) HIRSCH LIEBMANN was born on November 28, 1924, in Karlsruhe, Germany. After her father died, her mother kept his photography studio going. Hanne remembered that in the 1933 boycott of Jewish businesses, the windows of the studio were defaced with derogatory messages. In October of 1940, Hanne and her mother were deported to Gurs camp in France, where Hanne met and fell in love with Max Liebmann. Hanne was rescued by the OSE (Children's Aid Society) and hidden in a children's home in Le Chambon-sur-Lignon. Her mother was deported and killed in Auschwitz. In 1943,

Hanne escaped to Switzerland. She and Max reunited there; they married, had a daughter, and immigrated to the United States in 1946.

MAX LIEBMANN was born in Mannheim, Germany, on September 3, 1921. In October of 1940, while working at a job helping families emigrate, Max was told the offices were closing and all Mannheim Jews were being deported to France. Max and his mother were sent to Gurs. He escaped Gurs just before the first deportation and reached Switzerland, where he worked in a refugee camp. Max and Hanne Hirsch married on April 14, 1945, in Geneva. Max's postwar accomplishments include being a leader of the American Gathering of Jewish Holocaust Survivors established by Vladka and Benjamin Meed (whom we meet in Part Three).

ALFRED MORITZ was born on June 13, 1930, and lived with his younger brother, Ernest, and their parents in Becherbach, a village in southeastern Germany, where their father owned a store. The family made numerous attempts to avoid the Nazis, fleeing to relatives in Luxembourg, and then in France. Beginning in the fall of 1942, Alfred and Ernest were separated from their parents, and had to rely on strangers to keep them alive. Even in the most remote hiding spot, the boys were never free from danger.

KEY DATES IN PART TWO

1939 France sets up Gurs, in southwestern France, as a detention camp for refugees.

1940 On May 10, Germany attacks the Low Countries: the Netherlands, Luxembourg, and Belgium. Belgium was being reinforced by French and British troops, and on May 20, the Germans effectively cut off the Allies, forcing them to retreat.

An unexplained pause by Hitler enables Great Britain to evacuate around 340,000 soldiers from Dunkirk and another 220,000 from other French ports. Belgium surrenders on May 28.

German troops cross into France on May 13 and continue the assault. On June 12, the French premier, Paul Reynaud, is told the battle for France can't be won. He resigns on June 16.

World War I hero Marshal Philippe Pétain forms a new French government. On June 22, an armistice is signed dividing France into two zones. Germany occupies the north, while the southeast portion, based in Vichy, is the unoccupied zone. The Vichy government under Pétain cooperates—and collaborates—with the Nazis' persecution policies.

On October 22, 1940, 6,504 Jews from Mannheim and other regions of Germany are arrested and deported to Gurs, an internment camp in the unoccupied zone.

1941 The Vichy government takes all Jewish property for the state. Jews are also dismissed from civil service positions and barred from professions like law and medicine.

1942 Deportations of Jews from France begin at the end of March and accelerate through the summer. At first, only adults are sent, but later that summer whole families are deported. Most Jews who are French citizens aren't deported. The Catholic Church protests the deportations.

1943 Deportations, which had paused, start again in January 1943 and continue until August 1944.

1944 On June 6, D-Day, Allied troops under the command of General Dwight D. Eisenhower invade Normandy. The Germans surrender Paris on August 25, 1944. The French resistance continues to aid the Allies. The French resistance has helped prepare the way, conducting sabotage, helping Jews and Allied soldiers escape, and providing Jews with false documents.

This propaganda map depicts Nazi Germany at the height of its domination over Europe. Entitled "The new Europe is unbeatable," it shows German territorial gains and offensive movements of its army, navy, and air force against its enemies in 1942. By that time, Germany had made alliances with Finland, Italy, Bulgaria, and Hungary and had conquered France, Norway, and every European nation in Eastern Europe. The German invasion of the Soviet Union had pushed nearly into Moscow. Meanwhile, Britain was fighting to maintain its presence in Africa and the Middle East. At this point, the United States, which entered the war in December of 1941 after Japan bombed Pearl Harbor, had not yet had an impact.

Chapter Five

ALFRED: THE CRIME OF BEING DIFFERENT

TWO BROTHERS ON THE RUN IN FRANCE

Absolutely no one could be trusted.

"The thugs threw everything throwable to the street. As dusk fell, looters appeared," said Alfred Moritz. He was remembering Kristallnacht, the pogrom that took place in November of 1938, when he was eight.

Alfred and his brother, Ernest, who was two years younger, lived with their parents in Becherbach, a village in southwest Germany close to the borders of Luxembourg and France. The Moritzes could trace

Ludwig Moritz, Alfred's father, stands in front of his store in pre-1933 Becherbach, Germany.

family roots in the area back to the 1700s and felt part of the community. Friends watched out for Ernest as he explored the neighborhood to help lead a cow to water or sit on a plow. Ludwig Moritz, the boys' father, had fought in World War I alongside his best friend, Julius Klein, a local carpenter.

On Kristallnacht, as Nazi thugs roamed the town terrifying Jewish families, Julius Klein took a stand. He planted himself in front of the Moritz house, a three-pronged pitchfork in hand, daring any SS brownshirts to get past him.

"He announced that anyone touching anything would find himself with a prong or two in his/her belly. He stood guard all night, ashamed, he said later, to be born German," Alfred recalled. Mr. Klein, Alfred said, was "a tough old bird," loyal and brave.

That kind of loyalty was rare. Alfred's own best friend, Adi, joined the Hitler Youth group. Alfred couldn't forget looking out the window to see Adi parading in front of his house with other schoolmates, all of them singing antisemitic songs.

"I was overwhelmed by shock, I was perplexed . . ." Alfred said. "If Adi could do such a thing, then it was true that absolutely no one—absolutely no one—could be trusted."

Alfred's father told his son not to pay attention. Ludwig Moritz and his brothers had fought for their country in World War I. In fact, Alfred had been named in memory of an uncle killed in World War I. But, of course, this service and dedication meant nothing to Hitler's extreme antisemitic regime. The Nazis targeted living Jews and the dead. In 1942, the Nazis ordered Alfred's name removed from a local war monument honoring fallen heroes.

After Kristallnacht, Alfred's father was detained for three months in Dachau concentration camp, which had been opened in 1933 as a detention center for political prisoners. He withstood brutal conditions and was released only after agreeing to turn over his dry-goods store to a Nazi sympathizer.

The Moritz family tried to escape to the United States. Although this paperwork didn't come through in time, they were able to get visas for nearby Luxembourg, where they had relatives. However, when Germany invaded Luxembourg on May 10, 1940, they had to flee. Since the Moritzes also had family connections in France, Alfred's cousin Réne drove them there. They joined a long procession of refugees, some in cars, others on foot, on bicycles, or in horse-drawn carts.

France had welcomed Jews after World War I. However, by 1939, the French had begun to impose limits on immigration and set up camps to detain refugees. The USHMM estimates that by the time Alfred's family arrived, there were as many as 350,000 Jews in the country, and less than half were French citizens.

Alfred and Ernest Moritz and their cousin Réne from Luxembourg. When Germany invaded Luxembourg in May of 1940, Réne drove the Moritz family to France.

As Alfred and his family slowly made their way south on the clogged road, they were stopped at a roadblock in Dijon. Alfred's father was arrested as an alien enemy and taken even farther south. He was imprisoned at a former tile factory called Camp Les Milles. Alfred's mother and the two boys were allowed to pass and made it to the village of Sainte-Lizaigne, where their father's sister lived.

Their aunt found them a place in the home of two retired schoolteachers. For a while at least, the boys and their mom were safe. Yet the long tentacles of Nazi oppression would touch them again.

In their attempts to flee the Third Reich, Alfred and his family had been swept up in the relentless onslaught of Nazi aggression. Germany had annexed Austria in 1938; Hitler's invasion of Poland on September 1, 1939, led the British to declare war two days later. A few months later, Hitler set his sights north, invading Denmark and Norway on April 9, 1940. The invasion of the Low Countries (Belgium, Luxembourg, and the Netherlands) followed in May.

Allied British and French forces were providing support to Belgium, which surrendered on May 28, 1940. German troops had moved to the rear to encircle Allied troops. To avoid total defeat, the British had to retreat. Between May 26 and June 4, British ships of all shapes and sizes evacuated approximately 338,000 troops from Dunkirk, France. It would be four long years later before the Allies returned to France, storming the beaches of Normandy on D-Day, June 6, 1944, and beginning the final campaign to defeat Hitler's forces.

The 1940 British retreat left the French alone; on

June 5 of that year, the Battle of France began. By June 14, German troops had entered Paris. It was declared an "open city," meaning that the defenders gave up, but the occupying force agreed not to destroy it. Marshal Philippe Pétain, who replaced the former prime minister, decided to collaborate and seek an agreement with Germany.

Under the terms of the Franco-German Armistice of June 22, 1940, France was divided into two zones:

> **Occupied France:** This portion of the country was under German military occupation, often referred to simply as Occupied France. General Charles de Gaulle, who escaped to England, became the leader of the Free French and formed a government in exile.

> **Vichy France:** The unoccupied zone was under nominal French control through Pétain's authoritarian Vichy government, which collaborated with Germany. This unoccupied zone was made up of the southeastern two-fifths of the country, with its capital in Vichy, a city in central France.

The collaboration of the Vichy government with the Nazis would have severe repercussions for Jewish families, including French citizens and thousands who'd escaped to France as refugees. Then, in October of 1940, the Nazis also rounded up the Jewish population of several German provinces. Entire families were put on trains and sent to internment facilities in France including camps at Les Milles (where Alfred's father was imprisoned); Gurs, in the south near the Spanish border; and Rivesaltes, also in the south closer to the Mediterranean Sea.

Beginning in 1942, the Vichy government allowed the Nazis to pursue their horrific policies even further: Innocent Jewish men, women, and children were sent from these camps on transports that eventually reached Nazi death camps in Poland.

A PEACEFUL INTERLUDE

Alfred, Ernest, and their mother felt fortunate to be living in Sainte-Lizaigne with Hélène and Marthe Foerster, the two unmarried sisters. The former teachers made sure the boys attended school, where the teachers were supportive. Alfred and Ernest learned French quickly with the help of children's books. They liked *Alice's Adventures in Wonderland* and the stories of Jules Verne. Their ability to speak French would turn out to be essential to their survival.

Soon everyone in the village recognized the blond brothers as they explored the orchards, picked fresh strawberries in the fields, or tagged alongside a farmer and his horse plowing a field. Best of all, said Alfred of their new friends, "Their kindness gave us again some confidence in human goodness."

GO AWAY WITH THOSE CHILDREN

But this interlude of safety didn't last. As part of its cooperation with Nazi Germany, the Vichy government began to implement antisemitic regulations. This included registering Jews and collecting information on where they lived—a first step that, for many, eventually led to deportation to Drancy, an internment camp near Paris. Beginning in June of 1942, Drancy served as a transit camp to send Jews on to their deaths at Auschwitz or Sobibor.

As part of the new regulations, Alfred, Ernest, and their mother were ordered to register at a local office. "We found ourselves in a yard surrounded by high walls, together with a large number of other similarly mandated persons—all of whom turned out to be Jews," Alfred recalled. The fact that those waiting were Jewish women and children was disturbing, since registrations could be used to "trap unsuspecting people and make them 'disappear.'"

As they waited in line, a woman who worked in the building approached. Beckoning to Alfred's mother, she led her and the boys through a deserted corridor and back outside.

Alfred remembered her words: "'Go away with those two beautiful children,' she told our mother as we left. Without any doubt, this person saved our lives."

In the winter of 1942, another intervention saved Alfred's father, who was still living in horrible conditions at Les Milles, the former tile factory, where red-brick dust covered everything. He and some other prisoners were released under the pretext that they were seriously ill, giving Alfred's father another chance to avoid deportation. When Alfred went to meet his dad at the train station in the village, he hardly recognized the thin, gaunt man his father had become.

Alfred's family had to find a new place to live since the retired schoolteachers couldn't accommodate the entire family. Alfred remembered wandering the village, his parents pushing Ernest in a wheelbarrow because he was sick and too weak to walk. Eventually, they found an icy, abandoned cottage.

A few months later, transports started. "On July 4, 1942, the Vichy Government agreed to the deportation of all non-French Jews from the South Non-occupied Zone [Vichy zone]," wrote Alfred.

It was clear: They could no longer live openly in a cottage where others could see them. The family needed a safe place to hide, and a way to get food. They decided to go to the nearby town of Issoudun, where Mr. Moritz's youngest brother, Jacques (formerly Jakob), had moved in 1935. Alfred's mother and little brother took the train. Mr. Moritz wanted to avoid being seen in public, so he and Alfred walked ten miles through the fields. While their parents made do in a hayloft on their uncle's property, Alfred and Ernest were sent to stay with a seamstress in a nearby village.

Pumpkins, recalled Alfred, were about all they had to eat. "After a few weeks of non-stop pumpkin soup, pumpkin pie, pumpkin salad, pumpkin ratatouille etc., our parents heard of a Jewish organization which harbored children, either smuggled out of the internment camps at Gurs and Rivesaltes or left behind by their parents."

That group was called OSE, which stands for Oeuvre de Secours aux Enfants [Children's Aid Society]. This relief organization was founded in 1912 by Russian Jews to help Jews suffering from religious persecution and took on resistance and rescue work in France during World War II. (OSE remains active today as a Jewish organization dedicated to health, education, and social work.)

OSE in France served as both a relief organization and an underground rescue effort. Working with the Vichy government, OSE was able to secure the release of some Jewish children from internment camps such as Gurs and Rivesaltes, so long as their parents agreed. The children were then cared for in OSE children's homes, which operated openly. Often that was just the first stop. From there, OSE worked to provide some of the children with new identities and moved them into hiding through an underground network. OSE also smuggled teens over the mountains out of France to safety in Switzerland.

OSE also accepted children whose parents were in hiding. A man who was taking his own children to an

Children play basketball outside Château Le Masgelier, an OSE-run children's home. This is where Alfred and Ernest Moritz stayed. One of the building's turreted towers is visible in the picture.

OSE home for safety offered to bring Alfred and Ernest too. The boys traveled to an OSE children's home located at Château Le Masgelier, a castle in central France. Since Ernest was still weak from illness, he was placed in quarantine in a turret room and given extra food to build his strength.

"ERNEST BUTTER"

Like the good little brother he was, Ernest shared his special ration of butter with Alfred. "He scraped the butter from his bread, wrapped it in a piece of paper, and let it down, attached to a string, from the window," recalled Alfred. "A few of us ragamuffins managed to steal a few potatoes in a nearby field, and making a fire as I had watched the farmer do in Becherbach [his hometown back in Germany], we roasted the potatoes which we then ate with a dab of 'Ernest butter.'"

Yet even here the brothers weren't safe. In reflecting on the increased persecution of Jews in France in 1942, Alfred later remarked, "It was decided that inasmuch as Jewish children posed a threat to German Aryan racial purity, they were henceforth also to be exterminated."

When two men in uniform arrived to question Alfred and Ernest and ask about their parents' whereabouts, OSE staff decided the brothers needed to be moved to a more remote location.

The boys were sent first to the city of Limoges to a children's home. OSE and the French underground then provided false identity papers and ration cards. The brothers became Alfred and Ernest Mauricet, French citizens: two innocent, non-Jewish boys on their own, unfortunately separated from their parents by the war.

They would need those papers—and their ability to speak French. Because to reach their next hiding place, Alfred and Ernest would have to embark on a treacherous journey.

COULD IT BE A TRAP?

Travel using false papers was dangerous, even for children. Escorted by an OSE volunteer, the Moritz brothers and two Jewish girls were brought to the railway station in Limoges. There they got their first scare.

The station café was full of German soldiers. As Alfred watched in dismay, a soldier motioned to his cute little brother with a sugar cube, an irresistible temptation to a hungry boy. It seemed like an innocent, friendly gesture. It might just as easily be a trap for Ernest.

"Our woman escort hissed—without moving her lips, it seemed—'Don't move, walk away slowly,' and we all left the café in a manner so nonchalant that any casual observer could not detect that these people had something to hide."

Even a casual encounter like this could mean discovery and capture. "The fear had been, of course, that this German would have pulled the boy's pants down to see if he was circumcised, hence Jewish," Alfred explained.

They made their way to the station platform. As they were about to board the train, a young man appeared. He was their next escort. The children ignored him. They'd been issued a strict warning in advance: No matter what happened, they should pretend not to know him. They shouldn't even look at him.

"He belonged to the 'Garel group,' a group organized by Georges Garel (Grigori Garfinkel), known for his courage and daring, who had been picked from the French underground for these OSE smuggling missions," said Alfred.

Garel, a French engineer born in what is today Lithuania, set up a secret network within OSE and is credited with saving 1,500 children. This operation, Alfred reflected later, "took both daring and guts."

Surrounded by German soldiers on the train, Alfred looked with longing at the men's snacks. "They ate delicious-looking rye-bread sandwiches carried in kidney-shaped tin boxes," he recalled. The bread reminded Alfred of the kind his grandmother in Becherbach used to bake. "We tried to look our hungriest in the hope that they would share their food—of course, they did not."

The children and their secret escort arrived at Toulouse in the evening. The young man quietly ordered them to remain at the station until someone arrived to tell them what to do next. Then he disappeared. The four children waited. And waited. Still no one came.

They ended up spending the night alone, growing hungrier by the hour. Alfred said, "Wandering about the station entrance in the rain, we came upon a vendor of sausages. I recall the delicious aroma. We had no money and he did not take pity, despite our hangdog looks."

At last, in the morning, a woman arrived to help them continue their journey through southern France. They boarded another train, spent the night in a hotel with just some cheese to eat, and then climbed on a run-down, rickety bus into the Cévennes, a mountainous region in south-central France. Again the children had a close call: Two soldiers boarded to check papers. Fortunately, their escort had placed them in the last row, and the soldiers lost interest before reaching them.

By this time, Alfred and Ernest, who were thirteen

and eleven, were exhausted and starving. Still the bus kept rumbling along, farther and farther into the countryside, which Alfred called "a wild land of goats, chestnuts and bramble."

The landscape seemed so remote Alfred began to breathe easier, hoping this meant they would now be out of reach of all those "thugs with obviously sick minds who were hunting them down, and wanted to do them in, for the simple reason that these little boys were breathing the same air as everyone else, on this planet Earth."

At long last, the four children arrived at a remote hilltop village called Vernoux-en-Vivarais, in a mountainous area of south-central France. Italy lay to the east and Switzerland to the northeast.

Everyone in the area seemed to know their escort. She was apparently a frequent visitor who pretended to be a social worker looking after children who had been wards of the state. Only the village priest knew the truth: The children were Jews in hiding. (According to Alfred, the priest, Father Riou, was later arrested for underground activities and deported, but survived the war.)

Their new life was about to begin. A tenant farmer named André Aubert took Alfred and Ernest in his cart to his widowed mother's cottage. The two girls went off with his brother, a miller. Extra money was welcome in this poor region, and OSE paid the villagers a little to help care for the children.

The brothers would now live with a peasant widow in her small cottage on a hillside. Alfred said, "The house was divided into two sections, with two cows, a pig and goats occupying one half, keeping the house warm with their body-heat in winter while ensuring a variety of strange new smells and flies, in the warmer months."

There was no electricity; the only heat came from a large fireplace. The boys were kept busy helping the widow with chores, including long hours gathering wood for heat and cooking. Food was meager and they always felt hungry. They ate chestnuts in season, and gathered mushrooms from the nearby forest to eat fried in oil with garlic. During potato harvest season, Alfred was loaned out to work on other farms and paid with a welcome sack of potatoes.

The boys attended the local school, and because they were masquerading as Christians, they went to church and Sunday school too. The school was three or four miles away. "Barefoot in our straw-filled clogs, we ran through the woods to attend school in the mornings and most days returned to tend to the farm animals in the afternoon."

Like Alfred and Ernest Moritz, brothers Isaac and Bernard Lajbman hid from the Nazis in the French countryside. In this 1943 photo, they cuddle two sheep in the village Tourinnes-Saint Lambert, where they were living in hiding with separate families. Their parents survived in Belgium using false papers and the family was reunited.

Danger lurked even in this remote place. "Our teacher, Mr. Gounod, was unhappy with this part-time attendance and threatened to denounce us if we did not improve our school attendance," said Alfred. "He did not make clear to whom and for what he would denounce us, although we immediately understood his meaning."

Another time, the boys happened to find two pairs of swimming trunks near a waterfall pool and donned them to swim. When two nuns from a children's home located nearby suddenly appeared to claim the clothes, Alfred and Ernest froze. Had the bathing trunks been left there on purpose to trap them?

"Here we were, naked as the day we were born, forced to undress under the prying eyes of the nuns and with the snickering of the kids in our ears. The event was traumatic, as the cardinal rule for potential survival was, for boys, never, ever, ever to show one was circumcised," Alfred said. Fortunately, nothing came of the incident.

Elsewhere, as crackdowns and raids accelerated, OSE smuggled some children, especially older teens, out of France into Switzerland. Alfred and Ernest remained in the village, although they began to feel a growing sense of dread.

Sometimes, Alfred felt threatened by potential informers. His teacher continued to frighten him, telling Alfred about a bounty system for the denunciation of hidden Jews. "He said he knew who I really was, and he would claim the bounty unless I did my homework." Another time, a woman arrived at the cottage and, along with the widow, screamed at the boys to admit the truth of who they were, all in the hope of claiming a reward.

"We didn't cry, remained calm, but denied everything. . . . The bounty huntress left in a huff, indicating that she was not through with us yet; she would return shortly, with some mean big men, who would know how to make nasty little boys talk." Alfred had no idea if his father was still alive, but thought he would have been proud of them.

"The rapid advance of the liberating Allied forces put an end to this very close brush with certain death," wrote Alfred later.

He and Ernest survived in that mountain village for eighteen months. On June 6, 1944, the Allies invaded Normandy. Paris was liberated by August 25 of that year. Although the war wasn't yet over, in October of 1944, OSE contacted their aunt in Sainte-Lizaigne, providing their address. The boys were able to write. And then something miraculous happened: They received a letter from their parents, whom they hadn't seen in a year and a half.

Ernest wrote back, "'We were very surprised in getting this letter. But now, we are waiting for the day when you will come and get us. We are in good health, we got taller and bigger. We're on a farm . . . We are with a widow, kind of old. Here there are chestnuts and apples of which we eat a lot.'"

REUNION

As it happened, the boys would have to travel to meet their parents. OSE helped arrange the reunion. An older teen would take the boys by train to Lyon. From there, they'd travel on their own to Châteauroux, a town not far from their aunt's village.

By now, Alfred and Ernest had been through so much that traveling alone didn't bother them. They were even asked to watch over another boy about their own age. The three were told to stay in the waiting room at the Châteauroux station until their families arrived.

They sat on a hard wooden bench for what seemed a very long time. Then the parents of the other boy arrived, screaming and waving their arms in excitement. Alfred and Ernest considered themselves above such undignified displays. They had become "self-sufficient, hardened and emotionally tough; for our part, we had learned, the hard way, to always keep our emotions in check and had no patience with such behavior."

A little while later, a lone woman entered the waiting room and also began to scream. She seemed even more hysterical and emotional than the people who'd just left.

Alfred later wrote in his memoir (in all caps): "WE THEN REALIZED THAT THIS PERSON WAS OUR MOTHER!"

After the war, the Moritz family settled in Sainte-Lizaigne, where

Ernest (left) and Alfred Moritz (right) pose with their friend Georges (center) in a field in France after the war, in September of 1945.

both boys attended secondary school in nearby Issoudun. Alfred and Ernest later immigrated and graduated from universities in the United States.

The Moritzes were the rare Jewish family who survived. Alfred learned later that most of the members of his mother's family, including his maternal grandmother and aunt, were killed. Another aunt and uncle, along with their five children, the youngest only nine years old, were also murdered in the Holocaust.

But how did Alfred's parents escape the Nazis? Where had they been during the long months when Alfred and Ernest were chopping wood in a remote village?

With their sons under the care of OSE, Klara and Ludwig Moritz made one unsuccessful attempt to escape into Switzerland. The smuggler couldn't be trusted, so instead they managed to get false papers as citizens of Luxembourg. They then found an unlikely hiding place: a mental health asylum in the south of France where paying guests masqueraded as inmates to hide from the Germans. Alfred's mother knit for local families in exchange for extra food, while his father tended the vegetable garden.

However, their money was running out and they worried about having to leave. One day, Ludwig Moritz, now known as Mr. Meschler from Luxembourg, made what could have been a fatal mistake. A fellow inmate, a well-to-do French woman, mentioned that she knew

Luxembourg well, as she'd often been there to visit a dear friend named Tony Wolf.

What a coincidence! Before he could stop himself, Mr. Moritz exclaimed that Tony Wolf was his sister. The woman hardly knew what to think. She'd been at Tony's wedding, she said, and she was absolutely sure her friend's maiden name was Moritz, *not* Meschler.

Ludwig Moritz had to admit the truth: Moritz was indeed his real name. His mistake turned out to be a lucky one. Instead of informing on Alfred's parents, the French woman became a good friend and saved them. She paid for Mr. and Mrs. Moritz to remain at the asylum until the fall of 1944, when France was liberated. "After the war, our parents scrimped and saved enough so that, in due course, they were able to repay their generous benefactor," Alfred recalled.

Alfred Moritz went on to become a successful architect in the Washington, DC, area. He married, had two children, and was an accomplished artist and proud grandfather. Alfred died in 2011 at the age of eighty. His brother, Ernest, settled in Florida. Ernest was married for fifty years. He was a successful businessman and father of four sons before passing away at age seventy-eight in 2010.

Alfred might never have recorded his incredible story

of survival had it not been for an incident in 1994. He happened to see a newspaper photo of a refugee in the Balkan conflict. (Also called the Yugoslav Wars, these conflicts between 1991 and 2001 resulted in the death of an estimated 130,000 people or more.)

In the photo, a man was pushing a wheelbarrow with his belongings through the snow, with a scrawny dog in the distance. "I felt a shock," wrote Alfred. "The scene took me back over half a century, to a time when my parents, looking for an abode, were forced to push my nine-year-old brother Ernest through just such a snowy landscape as he was too ill and weak to walk. They resembled this poor man, because just as he, they had committed the unpardonable crime of being different."

LOOK, LISTEN, REMEMBER: David Moritz, Alfred's son, helps to keep Alfred's illustrated memoir of his World War II experiences available online at http://www.survivalinwwii.com/en/01.html. In 2010, Alfred was a guest speaker at the United States Holocaust Memorial Museum. You can listen to Alfred's voice and find an audio recording of that event here: https://collections.ushmm.org/search/catalog/irn598422.

Erinnerungen

an

Camp de Gurs

Page from the memoirs of Camp de Gurs illustrated by Eva Liebhold. Eva's artwork depicts daily life in the camp, including people cooking, bathing, and hanging laundry. Eva was born in Mannheim, Germany, in 1921 and was deported with her family to the Gurs concentration camp in France in October of 1940. Eva and her mother were sent to Auschwitz in 1942, where they were murdered. Her father was also killed. Eva's younger brother, Werner, born in 1927, was the only family member to survive. He was hidden by the relief organization Oeuvre de Secours aux Enfants (OSE), and later fought in the French resistance.

Chapter Six

MAX: MY SHOES BECAME SHREDS

OVER THE MOUNTAINS TO FREEDOM—AND LOVE—IN SWITZERLAND

All of a sudden we heard voices behind us: "HALT!"

Max's guide to freedom was a boy, just ten or eleven years old. When Max's train pulled into a village station in France, he was waiting, ready to help four young Jewish people make a dangerous escape into Switzerland. If they were caught before they reached the border, the boy's young age would not protect him.

The next morning they set off over the mountain. "We climbed all day, it started to rain, and when night came we were lucky to find a rock overhang which would keep us dry," said Max. They began again at dawn. Max had some sugar to eat, but no other food. At midmorning, the boy stopped and told the group they had to go on alone, down over the rocks to safety—they hoped. It was just as possible the Swiss might send them back.

Max's shoes were worn to threads. Hours later, they reached a road and began walking. That's when Max heard the command: "'HALT!'"

It had already been a long and harrowing journey for Max Liebmann. Max was born on September 3, 1921, in Mannheim, Germany. Max's father, Alfred, was part owner of a business that represented textile manufacturers. He made a good living and was able to afford cello lessons for Max, who began playing at the age of eight.

Under Hitler, Max reflected, "It did not take too long before life in school became more difficult for Jewish students." His former friends began to join the Hitler Youth. In 1934, while in high school, Max decided to fight back against the abuse heaped on the Jewish students. He took on one of his classmates who'd been bullying him. "The result of this fight was very dramatic," he recalled. "From that day on, harassment of Jews in my class ceased."

His fellow students may have backed down, but Max

couldn't stop a teacher from falsely accusing him of plagiarism. And there was nothing Max could do when he was kicked out of the school orchestra for being Jewish. It would be impossible, he was told, for a Jewish student to play Germany's national anthem.

"We were constantly under great pressure," Max said. "Neither my Jewish friends nor I went to our parents with the problems we encountered in the streets. Our parents had enough everyday worries: the economic situation became even more critical."

By 1937, Max had given up his dream of enrolling in a music conservatory. He started at a business school to learn languages, but after 1938, he was banned from all non-Jewish schools. Meanwhile, in March of 1938, his father left to pursue a job as a textile representative in Greece. Max never saw his father again. German competitors got wind of Alfred Liebmann's work in Greece. He fled illegally to France, but was eventually captured, deported to Auschwitz, and murdered.

Max was now working for an organization that helped Jews emigrate. On October 21, 1940, he was suddenly sent home. The manager closed the office, announcing that the Gestapo had informed him all Mannheim Jews were being deported from the country the following day.

When Max went home to let his mother know, she didn't believe him at first. Yet it was true. "The next

The Gurs internment and transit camp in France, around 1940–1941.

morning two police officers rang our bell, and told us that we were under arrest," said Max. Max and his mother were given an hour to pack. When the men returned, his mother had to sign over the apartment and all its contents to the government.

They were brought to the train station, where they found hundreds of other Jews in the same situation. "With very few exceptions everybody regardless of age was included, from newborns to the very old in their nineties."

GURS

After a long, slow journey, the train arrived at Camp de Gurs in France on October 25, 1940. Max was put into a barracks for men. Conditions were horrible, with more than 10,000 people crowded together.

"There were 25 barracks to a block, 60 people in one barrack, one small electric bulb at each end of the barrack, in the middle a stove and a small table. The stove did not help, we had no wood," Max recalled. They were given straw to sleep on. There were no chairs. The latrines were simply holes in a raised cement platform.

"People were demoralized," said Max. People were in shock. They'd gone from the comforts of their own private homes to crowded, filthy barracks infested by lice, bedbugs, rats, and mice. "Medical problems began in earnest, there was a dysentery epidemic, there was typhus and other diseases; we started to
lose people daily as a
consequence."

Max's mother was
able to work as a camp
clerk and Max some-
times got a pass, or
ticket, to visit her in
her office. One day
when he was there,
Max met a sixteen-
year-old girl named
Hanne Hirsch who was

View of a barrack in the Gurs internment camp in 1939.

helping as a messenger. He offered to walk with Hanne to get rations from the Swiss Red Cross barracks. And that's how it began.

In an interview years later, Hanne described her attraction to the skinny teen. "'There was no privacy for dating, but we saw each other every day,' she recalled. 'Max was allowed unlimited tickets to visit other people because of the fact he was a musician . . . The conditions were horrible, but we [had] a cultural life, and I was attracted by Max's interpretation of music.'"

The French allowed some social service organizations to operate in the camp. One group, to Max's delight, sent in musical instruments. Max joined a string quartet, which definitely impressed Hanne. Before long, the two had fallen in love.

Max and Hanne soon faced their first separation. In August of 1941, OSE (the organization that had saved Alfred and Ernest Moritz) approached Hanne's mother to say there were people in the French village of Chambon-sur-Lignon willing to help children and young people. If Hanne's mother gave her permission, OSE could arrange with Vichy government authorities to take charge of Hanne, which would enable her to leave Gurs camp.

View of the French village of Le Chambon-sur-Lignon. This village and the ones surrounding it were the site of an unusual community-wide rescue effort credited with saving about 5,000 Jewish people during the Holocaust. For these actions, many individuals, and the entire village of Plateau Vivarais-Lignon, were recognized by Yad Vashem as Righteous Among the Nations.

Protestant pastor André Tocmé, along with his wife, Magda, and his assistant, Pastor Edouard Theis, worked with villagers to hide Jews and provide false identity papers. The residents sheltered Jews in homes, farms, hotels, and schools. In some cases, they helped people cross the border into neutral Switzerland to safety.

Jewish children at the La Guespy children's home in Le Chambon-sur-Lignon, France, in the summer of 1942. OSE tried to save children from being deported from France to killing centers in Poland.

Max Weilheimer lights Hanukkah candles in the Gurs internment camp in France in 1941. It is the last photo of him before he was deported and murdered at Sobibor death camp. His wife, Lilly, died at Gurs in 1941. Max and Lilly had two sons, Richard and Ernest. The American Friends Service Committee (AFSC), a Quaker organization, worked with OSE to transfer fifty children from Gurs camp into an orphanage. In July of 1942, the brothers sailed to the United States, where each was taken in by one of their mother's sisters who lived only a block from each other.

Hanne recalled that her mother didn't urge her to stay, or even admit how desperately she would miss her daughter. Hanne said, "She loved me enough to let me go."

After Hanne left, Max was assigned a job running the office of the camp hospital. This enabled him to live in the hospital barrack, which provided better food as well as rooms with real beds.

In June of 1942, Max was also approached by the

OSE. His mother agreed to let him go, and he left the camp on July 25 for a Jewish Boy Scout camp near Lyon. A few days later, on August 1, Gurs was put on lockdown: No one was allowed to leave. Max said, "On August 6, the first train with 1000 people left Gurs for Drancy [a transit camp near Paris] and from there to Auschwitz."

There was an unexpected Jewish witness at the station that terrible day: a seventeen-year-old who risked her own safety to visit her mother. It was Hanne Hirsch.

Hanne had been safe in Le Chambon, hundreds of miles away. But when a cousin wrote to say that her mother was ill, Hanne decided to risk the dangerous trip back to Gurs. The lockdown meant Hanne could only see her mother from outside the barbed wire. They had to call out to each other across the barbed wire.

"'Two days later I saw her in the freight yard, where she was on a train waiting to be transported. She didn't know where she was going, but she knew she was not coming back. It was the last time I saw her.'" Hanne's mother was murdered at Auschwitz. A few months later, Max's mother met the same fate.

A WARNING

Hanne could have gone straight back to Le Chambon.

That would have been the wisest thing to do. But Hanne cared about Max, so she took another risk. She'd heard more raids by French police were expected, and she didn't think Max was safe at the scout training farm. After leaving Gurs, she made a detour to warn him.

Sure enough, within days of Hanne's visit, Max learned that a raid was expected. He hadn't been provided with false papers, so he and a friend decided to leave. They took sleeping bags and arrived at Le

Jewish youth living in the La Guespy children's home in Le Chambon-sur-Lignon, pose with the director, a Spanish physician named Juliette Usach. Hanne Hirsch, who later married Max Liebmann, is on the far right in the back row. In 1990, Usach was posthumously honored by Yad Vashem as Righteous Among the Nations for her work saving children during the Holocaust.

Chambon late at night. They camped out in a wooded area and slept undisturbed. Max kept wondering, "'Where can I find her?'"

Suddenly, Max and his friend heard a group of girls chatting as they walked through the woods. "Hanne was one of them!" said Max.

Hanne brought Max to the children's home, and then to meet Mme. Mireille Philip, a member of the French underground. She arranged for Max to stay in the hayloft of a farm owned by a family in the French resistance. Max joined the family for dinner and was able to get back some of his strength after being so malnourished during his time at Gurs.

A YOUNG GUIDE

After a stay of a few weeks, Max was brought back to Le Chambon, where members of the underground photographed him to prepare false identity papers. "Mme. Philip told me that I would be helped together with three other young people my age to escape to Switzerland."

The attempt would be treacherous. Even worse, there was no guarantee the Swiss would let them stay. They might be sent back to face the danger of arrest again. But with raids and the seizure of Jews escalating, it was worth the try.

"We went by train to St. Etienne and from there to a village close to St. Gervais in the French Alps. A 10 or

A group being smuggled out of France plows through snowdrifts on a rugged mountain pass in the Pyrenees in France sometime between 1942 and 1944. The group was rescued with the help of John Weidner's Dutch-Paris network. Weidner (1912–1994) was a Dutch Seventh Day Adventist who smuggled Jews, political refugees, and downed Allied airmen to Switzerland and Spain.

11 year old boy was waiting for us and brought us to his parents for the night. Early the next day we set out," said Max. They climbed all day, even once it began to rain. At night they found shelter beneath a rocky overhang.

The next morning, they kept on. Before noon, their young guide stopped and announced he was leaving them: They were on their own. Their descent over rocks would take them into Switzerland. The ascent had been difficult, but Max found going down even more difficult. Sharp rocks tore his thin shoes to shreds. Luckily someone had given him an extra pair, which he carried in his knapsack.

As they clambered down the slope, Max and the others stopped to bury their false identity cards, as they'd been instructed to do by the resistance. If the Swiss suspected they were part of an organized effort, they'd be more likely to be sent back to France. Max still had a German identity card—one marked with a J. He could only hope it might make the Swiss more sympathetic to his plight as a Jewish refugee seeking asylum.

They kept scrambling down the slope. Finally, hours later, they reached a road. That's when Max heard an order barked out from behind him: "'HALT!'" A Swiss military patrol had been watching their progress through binoculars. At first, Max was hopeful this would mean he was safe. It didn't. He and the others were held in a mountain hut overnight. The next morning, they were told they'd be escorted back up the mountain and would have to return to France.

However, as Max listened, it occurred to him that one of the officers was trying to send the refugees a very different message. The officer spoke in a loud, clear voice, listing one by one all the things Max shouldn't do. Suddenly, Max realized the man was actually trying to tell him something. The officer was giving them advice on how to try again—and not get caught by another patrol!

The patrol led them to the mountain summit and left them. Excitedly, Max blurted out to the others his theory about the officer's hidden message. Max wanted to try again and convinced another refugee to join him. The other two decided to head back to France. Max never knew what happened to them.

Max's second attempt worked. Following the officer's hints, Max and his companion found their way to a village without being stopped. Max's underground connections in Le Chambon had advised him to locate a Protestant or Catholic priest, which he did. Eventually, Max and his friend found their way to the Jewish community in Lausanne. Here they were told they would have to be turned in, but didn't need to worry about being sent back to France.

And that's what happened. Max spent the rest of the war in Swiss internment facilities. The conditions were much better than in France and he lived without fear of being deported to a death camp. He earned a low wage working to help refugee families and, of course, he kept in touch with Hanne. Best of all, on February 28, 1943, Hanne crossed illegally from France into Switzerland. Le Chambon had seemed safe, but Hanne was shaken by the memory of the train that had taken her mother away.

Max and Hanne were married on April 14, 1945, just weeks before the end of the war in Europe. Their daughter, Jeanne Evelyne, was born in 1946; the family immigrated to the United States in 1948.

"We arrived in New York with $70.00 in our pockets," said Max. "I started to work within a week after our arrival."

One of the first things he saved for was a new cello.

Max went on to earn a degree in accounting and to launch a successful business career; Hanne worked in a medical office. The couple has a grandson and two great-granddaughters. In April of 2018, Max and Hanne Liebmann, ages ninety-six and ninety-three, were interviewed on the occasion of their seventy-third wedding anniversary.

Remembering their reunion in Switzerland, Hanne said, "'We were so overwhelmed with the wonderfulness of being alive and realizing that we both had made it.'"

LOOK, LISTEN, REMEMBER: You can watch an interview with this extraordinary couple here at https://www.ny1.com/nyc/all-boroughs/news/2018/04/11 /two-holocaust-survivors-who-met-in-internment-camp -nearing-73rd-wedding-anniversary#.

RESCUING CHILDREN AT CHÂTEAU DE LA HILLE

Château de la Hille was a home for refugee Jewish children in southern France near the Spanish border. It housed about a hundred children who were originally from Germany and Austria and had sought refuge in Belgium. When the children and their rescuers were forced to flee that country, they eventually made their way to an abandoned building called Château de la Hille. Nineteen children were evacuated to the United States in 1941.

A child's drawing of Château de la Hille.

Georges Herz leads a pair of oxen on the grounds of Château de la Hille in the spring of 1944.

But in August of 1942, French police raided the home and arrested forty older children and planned to deport them to death camps. The Château's director, a Swiss nurse named Roesli Naef, sprang into action. She contacted a fellow Swiss relief worker named Maurice Dubois, who put pressure on the Vichy government to release the children. Roesli then worked to smuggle the older ones out of France into Spain or Switzerland. About ninety of the one hundred

Children peel potatoes at Château de la Hille sometime in 1943 or 1944.

children survived. Maurice Dubois and Roesli Naef were honored by Yad Vashem as Righteous Among the Nations for their rescue efforts.

Three young men pose for a photograph at the children's home of Château de la Hille, two years before they joined the French resistance. From left to right: Rudi Oehlbaum, Egon Berlin, and Joseph Dortort. Egon was killed in action in 1944 at age sixteen.

Chapter Seven

RUTH: THE FRAGILE LINK OF LETTERS

A FAMILY TORN APART BY THE HOLOCAUST

I do not believe I could have survived without this fragile link . . .

"The picture of the Führer [Adolf Hitler] was displayed everywhere, in schools, shops, offices," wrote Ruth David about growing up in Germany under the Nazi regime. "Gradually more and more men appeared in brown uniforms. They walked stiffly and threw out their arms in the 'Heil Hitler' greeting, which they made to sound like a hostile bark.

"Soldiers with rifles, or else with spades over their shoulders, marched to military music through the village, singing Nazi songs which were meant to frighten us with threats of 'Jewish blood dripping from our knives' and proud declarations: *'Heute gehört uns Deutschland, morgen die ganze Welt'* (Today Germany, tomorrow the World.)"

THE TERROR OF KRISTALLNACHT

Ruth Oppenheimer David was born in Frankfurt, Germany, on March 17, 1929, and was raised in Fränkisch-Crumbach, a village in the hilly, wooded Odenwald region of southern Germany. Her grandfather and father had been born there. Her family felt part of a welcoming community, but that changed once the Nazis came to power.

Ruth had two older half brothers, Werner and Ernst, an older sister named Hannah, and a younger brother and sister, Michael and Feo. In 1935, when the local school closed to Jewish children, Ruth and Hannah switched to a Jewish school in a nearby town. One day, when they were being driven in a van to school, a villager attacked them, breaking the windows. Soon their former friends stopped playing with them. The tentacles of Hitler's hatred of Jews had wormed their way into even the most remote areas of the country.

During Kristallnacht in November of 1938, brown-shirts attacked Ruth's home. Her elderly uncle, who was in a wheelchair, was thrown down a flight of stairs and his chair destroyed. Her father and brother Ernst were arrested and taken to Buchenwald concentration camp. Ernst had managed to get a visa to the United States and so he was let go. Her father was held for several months.

After that, hoping that a larger city would be safer and allow the family to be less conspicuous than in a small village, Ruth's mother got a job as a director of an orphanage in Mannheim, in central Germany.

"In Mannheim the synagogue had been destroyed by fire [on Kristallnacht], but there still remained a Jewish school that we were to attend," said Ruth. "This was the third school in my nine-year-old life . . . Many of my new classmates did not survive their childhood. In less than two years, they, with the rest of Mannheim's Jews, were among the first to be deported from Germany, an attempt to make the city *judenrein* (cleansed of Jews). . . .

"I was fortunate; I was not to be deported, but shocked when my parents announced at the beginning of June 1939 that I was to be sent to England . . . I had experienced enough to know that life was not going to improve for us, that we were in real danger. . . . I was keen to leave Germany now, but not alone and not for England.

"They gave me little warning, less than a week. . . . What little time I had on my own I spent looking despairingly into the vacant, unknown future, hoping above all that this banishment would be short."

Ruth's parents had found out about a rescue effort called the Kindertransport, through which about 10,000 Jewish children in Nazi-occupied countries were brought to safety, mostly to England. Ruth escaped on the Kindertransport in June of 1939.

She was sad to part from her family, and she would also miss their longtime housekeeper from her village home, a young Catholic woman named Mina Dümig. Against all odds, Mina had done her best to defy Nazi laws forbidding her to work for a Jewish family and remained fiercely loyal to Ruth's mother and the children she had grown to love.

Ruth did not expect to meet Mina again. But one day, nearly twenty years later, Ruth would find she owed Mina a tremendous debt.

Thanks to the Kindertransport, Ruth and her older sister, Hannah, were safe in England. Ruth's two older half brothers had also escaped, and were living in South America and the United States. But Ruth's parents, Moritz and Margarete Oppenheimer, along with their two youngest children, Michael and Feodora, were caught in Germany, unable to get visas to leave.

Ruth's mother tried to keep in touch with her four older children, who were now scattered across the globe. Her letters meant the world to Ruth, who was separated from Hannah and living in England in a girls' hostel with other Jewish refugees.

Once the war broke out in September of 1939, communication proved nearly impossible. Ruth tried to apply herself to her studies, but missed her parents desperately and worried about them. Her mother had given Ruth Mina's new address and encouraged her to stay in touch through a twenty-five-word Red Cross form. It was the only correspondence allowed between Germany and Allied countries. The forms had to pass inspection from censors and often took months to arrive.

And then Ruth got a shock: a real letter from her family. And it wasn't from Germany, but from France.

GURS CAMP

"Surprisingly, in the spring of 1941 I again had mail from my parents," said Ruth. "Even more surprisingly . . . it came directly, although it took some weeks, from the distant southwest corner of France, a little town called Gurs."

How had her family ended up in France? Along with the rest of the Jewish population in Mannheim, Germany, Ruth's parents and her two younger siblings, Michael and Feo, had been deported to Gurs, France, in October of 1940, just as Max Liebmann and his mother had.

Correspondence was allowed between Vichy France and England, although it was, of course, still censored. It gave Ruth hope to get news from her family again, though she was now old enough to realize her mother had to be careful in what she chose to reveal about their circumstances.

"In their letters, sent under the most utmost difficulties, my parents never mentioned the dreadful conditions in which they lived, nor the hunger and privations they had to endure... It was only years later that I discovered from survivors, whom I met or through reading their accounts, how impossible life was in the camps.

"Never did my parents mention their hunger, the cold or the constant threat of disease. Nor that they had to share a tiny space with too many others for sleeping and washing in insanitary [sic], primitive areas. They did not mention the filth, the stench, the lice and the rats."

Her family's stay in Gurs was only temporary. "In March 1941 my parents were taken with their youngest child, my little sister Feo, to Rivesaltes from Gurs. (Michael was already hidden with some of his peers from the camp, in a boarding school . . . near Toulouse.) By now even the French authorities realized that the conditions in Gurs were impossible," said Ruth.

Ruth's brother Michael had been rescued from Gurs by two Scandinavian helpers, Alice Resch and Helga Holbeck, who worked with the Quaker organization, the American Friends Service Committee. Michael Oppenheimer became Michel Olivier. By the summer of 1942, deportation raids in France accelerated, and Ruth credits Helga Holbeck with keeping her brother safe from detection.

"Conditions were also cruel at Rivesaltes, and squalor extreme," wrote Ruth later. "In the Mediterranean

Children in the Rivesaltes transit camp in southern France under the care of the OSE in 1942.

A Swiss Red Cross nurse named Friedel Reiter (later Friedel Bohny-Reiter) greets children as they arrive at the nursery school at the Rivesaltes internment camp sometime between 1941 and 1942. In 1942, she teamed up with Swiss educator August Bohny (whom she later married) to save hundreds of Jewish children by moving them out of the camp into children's homes and private residences. For their rescue efforts, Yad Vashem honored August and Friedel Bohny-Reiter as Righteous Among the Nations.

Roma (or Romani) children in Rivesaltes camp in France, sometime around 1941 or 1942. In addition to Jews, people of European Roma, or Romani, descent were considered ethnically inferior by the Nazis. Roma people in Europe, who originated from northern India, lived an itinerant lifestyle. The USHMM estimates that 250,000 Romas were killed during the Holocaust.

heat and near the salty swamps (*rives saltes*) there were swarms of mosquitoes and other insects which invaded the many barracks. There was barbed wire everywhere. At that time there were 3000 children in the Rivesaltes camp. Sixty babies died in a few months."

Ruth's parents had been unwilling to send their youngest children on their own to England, but now, like so many Jewish parents, they faced an impossible, heartbreaking decision. And, again, like others, they chose to entrust their beloved child to others in the hope that she could be saved.

"My younger sister Feo was left with my parents, but eventually, when a new opportunity of rescue arose, they let her go too. She was taken from the camp and looked after by an organization called Oeuvre de Secours aux Enfants (OSE, a Jewish resistance group)," said Ruth. "They brought her further north . . . and she lived with other displaced children in semi-hiding. This meant she was alone, separated from our brother Michael, with whom she had shared the horrors of the camp. She was seven years old."

A MOTHER'S ADVICE TO LIVE BY

Ruth wrote to her mother from England to say she could not imagine turning thirteen on her next birthday, in March of 1942. In the midst of her own suffering and fear, Ruth's mother gave her daughter words she would treasure all her life.

Her mother replied, "'It is nearly three years since we have seen each other and I am sure you have changed considerably. Through these hard times you have no doubt become a person of greater understanding, but I am sure you have remained my dear and good child. I am happy to know that you have a good friend. That is something to value. I have true friends and am very glad of them.'

"Still known as VE Day, Victory in Europe Day, May 8, 1945, should have been my mother's fifty-third birthday," wrote Ruth. "She was not to reach it. Her fiftieth was her last. We kept hoping for a long time . . .

Ruth Oppenheimer David.

"Accepting these deaths was difficult for all the hostel girls . . . Deep inside me I knew it was true, but spent years hoping and making up impossible stories of how my parents were perhaps lost somewhere, were ill and could not explain who they were, were unable to speak, or had forgotten where they once belonged. By some coincidence or miracle, we would find them one day. It was a vague and transient comfort, as daydreams are."

Ruth later discovered that her parents, Moritz and Margarete Oppenheimer, had been sent to Camp les Milles, and then to Drancy, on August 12, 1942. From there, they were part of Convoy 20, which departed for Auschwitz on August 17, arriving on August 19. Ruth learned that nine hundred people, including children, were gassed immediately.

Her brother, now known as Michel, and sister Feo survived the war and were later taken in by the Sommer family in Paris. Michel became a glassblower; Feo married a young rabbinical student from Tunisia and became known for her North African cooking, as well as being a loving wife and mother.

Ruth became a teacher and a mother of two. She published two books and traveled to Germany to talk about the Holocaust to young people. In 2012, Ruth was awarded the Order of Merit of the Federal Republic of Germany for her dedication to peace and commitment to Holocaust education.

The six Oppenheimer siblings never met all together again. In the 1950s, Ruth did meet Mina Dümig, her family's housekeeper, once more. At some point after Ruth left for England in 1939, Mina defied Nazi laws to join the family in Mannheim. But in October of 1940, when the Oppenheimers and their two youngest children were deported to France, Mina could accompany them no farther.

Before she left, Ruth's mother, Margarete, handed Mina a binder filled with family letters, including letters Hannah and Ruth had sent from England, along with ones from Ruth's older brothers, who were safe in Argentina and New York.

"Mother pushed an old file filled with letters into her arms and told her to keep them safe till she could hand them over to one of us. . . . Here were our family letters. Our only inheritance, handed to us by a very rare German Christian who had the courage to ignore the Nazi laws, regulations, propaganda and the terror," said Ruth. "In my understanding she was both one of the Righteous and a Saint."

Just as this book was going to print, I received a note from Ruth's daughter, Margaret Finch, to say that her mom had passed away from Covid-19 on April 6, 2020. Ruth's life, her compassion, and her incredible generosity inspired me to write this book and help to keep stories like hers alive. She will be missed.

LOOK, LISTEN, REMEMBER: Watch a news feature about Ruth David at home in Leicester, England, at the BBC, in which she speaks of the last letter she received from her mother when she was thirteen and her award from Germany for her work on Holocaust education: https://www.bbc.com/news/av/uk-england-leicestershire-19641062/leicester-woman-honoured-by-germany-for-holocaust-work.

PART THREE

Desperation and Defiance

True Stories from Poland

Around me there was so much pain that if it had been divided among everyone in the world, there would have been some left over.

—ADINA BLADY SZWAJGER,
doctor in the Warsaw ghetto

Children and families captured during the suppression of the Warsaw ghetto uprising (April 19, 1943–May 16, 1943) are forced to go to the Umschlagplatz (holding area near the railway station where people were assembled for deportation).

ABOUT THE PEOPLE IN PART THREE

PAULA BURGER was born in 1934 in Novogrudek (also Nowogródek), Poland, which today is part of Belarus. She lived with her parents and younger brother, Isaac. Her father, Wolf Koladicki, engineered a daring escape from the Novogrudek ghetto for his children. Paula and Isaac were taken to the forest, where a man named Tuvia Bielski led the famous Bielski Partisans, an armed resistance group determined to protect innocent men, women, and children.

BRONKA HARZ KURZ was born in Nadworna, Poland, on March 1, 1931. Today this is part of Ukraine. Her family tried to stand up to the occupying force—first the Soviets, then the Germans—but they were forced into the Kolomiya (or Kolomyja) ghetto. Bronka's short, handwritten memoir vividly describes the fears of a ten-year-old girl whose world is turned upside down.

WLODKA BLIT ROBERTSON and her twin sister, **NELLY BLIT**, born in 1931, were the daughters of two politically active parents in Warsaw, Poland. Their mother, Fela Herclich Blit, worked tirelessly to feed children in the Warsaw ghetto. She also found a way to smuggle the girls to safety on the other side of the wall.

BENJAMIN MEED was born Benjamin Miedzyrzecki in Warsaw in 1918. He escaped the Warsaw ghetto and joined the underground while living on the Aryan side of the wall. He and his future wife, Vladka Meed, helped plan and lead the Warsaw ghetto uprising. Passing as a non-Jew, he lived covertly outside the ghetto under the name Czeslaw Pankiewicz.

VLADKA MEED was born Feigele Peltel in Warsaw, Poland, on December 29, 1921. After her father's death, her mother, brother, and sister lived in the Warsaw ghetto until they were deported. Vladka spoke Polish and could pass as non-Jewish. When the resistance asked her to take on a dangerous role smuggling weapons into the ghetto, she agreed. She also protected children in hiding, including Wlodka and Nelly Blit. Vladka's unwavering courage and lifelong dedication to her community make her a hero, not just in her time, but in ours.

KEY DATES IN PART THREE

1939 On September 1, Germany invades Poland; Great Britain declares war on Germany on September 3. Warsaw, the capital of Poland, surrenders to Germany on September 27. Meanwhile, on September 17, the Soviet Union invades eastern Poland, effectively partitioning the country. Persecution of Polish Jews begins.

1941 Germany invades the Soviet Union, bringing all of Poland under Nazi occupation. Germans begin constructing concentration camps in Poland, which are used to kill six million Jews under the Final Solution policy. The Nazis also persecute and execute other groups, including homosexuals, Roma, and people with disabilities.

1943 Jews in the Warsaw ghetto stage an uprising to try to prevent the deportation of those remaining in the ghetto. The resistance continues nearly four weeks, from April 19 to May 16, before the ghetto is burned.

1944 In the city of Warsaw, the Polish Home Army, a resistance group, launches the Warsaw Polish uprising beginning in August of 1944. The hope that Soviet troops will intervene is not realized. In October, Germans retake the city. It's thought that about 166,000 civilians are killed, including 17,000 Jews. Many Poles are transported to concentration camps and the city is burned to the ground.

1945 Soviet forces arrive to capture Warsaw in January; German forces are driven out of Poland by March.

A Jewish partisan group in the Rudninkai Forest in Belarus sometime between 1942 and 1944.

Chapter Eight

PAULA: SURVIVAL IN THE FOREST

THE BIELSKI PARTISANS

We are lost, Papa. We are dead.

"A child can get lost watching the snow . . . the way it weaves and chases itself before collapsing to the ground," begins Paula Burger's memoir, *Paula's Window*. "I knew nothing about the war then. Snow fell, pure and sweet."

Paula Koladicki Burger was born in 1934. She lived on her family's farm outside Nowogródek in eastern Poland (today Novogrudek, Belarus), with her parents and little brother, Isaac (now Isaac Koll), who was born in 1939.

The area has a complicated history dating back

Yehuda Bielski, first cousin of the Bielski brothers (later known as Julius Bell when he immigrated to the United States), formed one of the most successful rescue and partisan groups of the war. Here he walks down a street in prewar Nowogródek. After July of 1941, when the city was taken over by the Nazis, Jews weren't allowed to walk freely and were forced to wear a Star of David badge on their clothes.

centuries. It has been fought over, especially by Poland and Russia, and has changed hands several times. In 1939, the region was invaded by the Soviet Union. Jewish families continued to live peacefully for a time. But that didn't last.

"Then, on a summer day in 1941, the sky exploded and our lives came tumbling down," Paula remembered. "I saw flashes on the horizon, leaving behind smoky red plumes like streaming fire. Planes flew so close that bullets scraped the ground right where I played."

The Nazis had arrived, and Paula would soon learn how cruel snow and cold could be, and how frightening it was to be lost.

TAKING THE GUESSWORK OUT OF HATE

Once the Germans arrived, in early July of 1941, they lost no time in imposing anti-Jewish laws. "Jews lost all citizenship rights. They handed over their valuables to the authorities. Jews could not walk on the sidewalks or streets. The Star of David we had to sew on our outer garments took the guesswork out of hate. Now we were easier to spot, and impossible to ignore," said Paula.

Paula rarely ventured out at all anymore and hid with her family on their farm. It wasn't safe to visit cousins or playmates; her parents were afraid to let their children out of their sight. With good reason. Almost immediately after taking control, the Nazis began deploying killing squads to round up Jews and murder people in cold blood.

Paula's father, Wolf Koladicki, was a successful business owner. He used his contacts to try to protect his family as the persecution of Jews intensified. He was able to get advance warning of roundups, death squads, and mass executions. "He knew when we had to run and when it was safe to return," Paula recalled.

Although exact numbers are hard to know, the USHMM estimates that between July 1941 and spring of 1942, "German authorities killed tens of thousands of Jews" in the region.

Thanks to her father, Paula's family managed to avoid having to move into the ghetto at first. For a time, they were able to hide with nearby Polish farmers, but after a few months they were betrayed. One night, men banged on the door and ordered them to report to the ghetto the next day. They had no choice but to obey. Nazis came for the family the next day and marched them to the Nowogródek ghetto.

"We could take only a few possessions," Paula recalled. "All I wanted was my doll. She was maybe six or seven inches tall and wore a pretty green party dress my mother had sewn."

Paula remembers trudging along with the rest of her family, her parents staring straight ahead. "Isaac bobbed up and down on my father's shoulders, laughing at the trees and rabbits."

Her little brother was too young to understand what was happening. But Paula feared what lay ahead. And so did her father. Paula later thought he must have already been trying to plot their escape.

Under heavy guard and surrounded by barbed wire and fences, the ghetto was a fearful, colorless place. "I can still see the decrepit buildings, the cramped room we shared with strangers, the strip of dead grass where I played," wrote Paula.

"My parents tried their best to convert madness into an acceptable routine. My father reported for his job (work detail) every day. My mother invented chores to divert our empty stomachs and restlessness." As they played hopscotch or hide-and-seek in the alley behind the apartment, Paula learned to stay as quiet as possible.

One day, her mother took her aside to make a request. "'If anything happens to me or your father, promise me you will take care of Isaac.'"

Even when Paula could no longer recall the sound of her mother's voice, those words stayed with her. Paula promised to do her best.

As time passed, more and more people in the ghetto were rounded up and deported. Rumors flew of massacres in nearby towns. Paula's father's work detail took him outside the ghetto. Sometimes he was gone for weeks at a time, and may have been able to use his contacts to gain more freedom of movement than most. However, eventually a Polish neighbor who coveted Mr. Koladicki's farm informed on him.

Nazi officers came to interrogate Paula's mother, demanding to know her husband's whereabouts. She did not know, but was nevertheless arrested and hauled away, leaving her seven-year-old daughter and three-year-old son in a ghetto apartment with an aunt.

Paula's aunt tried to comfort her, saying that her mother would probably return shortly. But Paula had seen others disappear from the ghetto: She knew enough to guess that her mother wasn't coming back. "I stopped asking about my mother because I knew she was dead," Paula said. "My mother was the wheel of my life. Without her, my world stopped turning."

Paula eventually learned that her mother, Sarah Ginienski Koladicki, who spoke both German and Polish, had been made to work as a translator for the Nazis for six weeks. Then she had been killed in September of 1942. Paula never discovered where her mother was buried.

NOW OR NEVER

One night, a man woke Paula and told her to dress quickly, bring Isaac, and follow him. "'I am taking you to meet a farmer. Do what he tells you and be silent as the grave. I know that what I ask of you is frightening, but your father is waiting on the other side [of the ghetto walls]. It's now or never.'"

Wolf Koladicki had arranged for his children to be smuggled out of the ghetto by a Polish farmer who brought barrels of water in and out. In the darkness, after the barrels were emptied, Paula and Isaac were ordered to climb into the wagon and hide inside one.

"To avoid discovery, we stayed in that dank coffin for endless hours," Paula remembered. "I held Isaac tightly in my arms so he wouldn't start crying.

"Just when I thought I couldn't take one more second, the wagon stopped. The farmer opened the barrel and gently extricated us. He led us to a dry barn, helped us up to the hayloft, and fed us hardboiled eggs, dark bread, and water."

That night, Paula lay awake, tense and worried, even though she was exhausted. She knew informers were paid for turning Jews over to the Nazis. However, this farmer, like other non-Jewish Poles in the area who assisted Jews trying to escape the ghetto, turned out to be a trustworthy friend. The next morning, he hid

Paula and Isaac under a pile of hay in his wagon. Paula was even more relieved when one of her cousins, who'd also managed to escape, sat up front, dressed like a peasant and pretending to be the farmer's wife.

The wagon creaked along, hour after hour. Finally, at twilight, the farmer stopped in the forest. Paula and Isaac's father was there to meet them. It was an emotional reunion. They hadn't seen him since their mother had been taken away.

"My father, ashen and overwhelmed, picked us up in his arms. . . . We wept for a courageous wife and mother who went to her death in our place."

THE BIELSKI BROTHERS

Paula's life in the Naliboki Forest began. Her father had joined the Bielski *Otriad*, or partisan unit, a secret armed group fighting against an occupying force. One of the most effective and inspiring Jewish resistance efforts of the entire war, the Bielski group is credited with protecting and rescuing more than 1,200 Jews, many of them women, children, and the elderly.

A postwar portrait of partisan Tuvia Bielski and his wife, Lilka.

The Bielskis were a large farming family with twelve children, ten sons and two daughters, who lived near Nowogródek. After their parents and two brothers were killed by the Nazis in December of 1941, three brothers, Tuvia (1906–1987), Asael (1908–1945), and Zus (1910–1995), fled to the forest. There they established a partisan unit led by Tuvia to fight back against the Germans and protect Jews. The youngest brother, Aharon (later Aron Bell),

Yehuda Bielski, first cousin of the Bielski brothers, poses with a large group of young children in the woods near Nowogródek in an undated prewar photo. According to the USHMM, Yehuda was serving as a lieutenant in the Polish army when he was wounded during the 1939 German invasion of Poland. He managed to make his way back home to Nowogródek. He later escaped the Nowogródek ghetto to join his cousins in the forest, providing valuable military expertise to the group. He is also credited with rescuing others from the ghetto.

born in 1927, was also a part of the group. Along with the four brothers, their first cousin, Yehuda Bielski (later Julius Bell, 1906–1994), affectionately known as the fifth brother, was also integral to the group's success.

Paula first caught sight of Tuvia Bielski atop a magnificent chestnut horse, "a statuesque, handsome man with wavy dark hair, a mustache, and shiny boots . . . Even off his horse, Tuvia Bielski was a giant of a man."

Although Paula's father possessed a gun, as his children's sole surviving parent, he avoided participating in the group's more dangerous military attacks. Instead, he devoted himself to missions to obtain food from local farms to feed the refugees. "Far less dangerous than blowing up bridges, it was still a risky enterprise," said Paula. "We lived in a forest infested with enemies."

The partisans relied heavily on local farms. Recalled Paula, "Tuvia ordered the partisans to demand enough food to survive but to refrain from greed. Some Poles obliged willingly. Others handed over the food, waited until it was safe, and then contacted the Nazis."

Tuvia Bielski's group also conducted sabotage, blowing up railways and destroying bridges. The members carried out operations against collaborators, informers, and others who persecuted and killed Jews. But Tuvia Bielski aimed to save Jews from the

According to USHMM, most of the members of the Bielski group involved in military actions were men. This is a postwar portrait of two of the few female Bielski Partisans who carried weapons. Pictured are Esther (Essie) Shor (a cousin of the Bielski brothers) and Itka Ass.

The sleeping car of a German train lies next to the tracks where it was derailed by the Polish resistance in 1943. Polish peasants helped Jewish families escape to the Bielski group, which also procured weapons from Russian partisan groups fighting against the Germans.

ghetto and keep them hidden. For this reason, since it was more than a fighting unit, the Bielski group accepted all who wanted to join, including children and the elderly.

Their ultimate goal was survival.

In the beginning, Paula enjoyed some of what life in the forest had to offer. She studied Hebrew with her father and sometimes played cards and checkers. Paula later became an artist, and loved the ever-shifting colors and shadows of the woods.

"The artist in me began studying nature: how a slice of blue sky split and slipped through the pine trees; a green spinning wheel painting the bushes; the wet texture of leaves glistening in the sunshine. Whenever I forgot the hateful world that brought me to this place, I appreciated the Naliboki's beauty."

At the same time, fear, cold, and hunger soon became the children's constant companions. Living conditions were primitive; Paula and Isaac had arrived sometime in the fall of 1942. "One morning I opened the tent to a white wonderland of snow," said Paula. "Winter had arrived. My father joined the men in building *zemlyankas,* or log bunkers. Built deep into the cold earth, they were accessible by ladders made of tree branches."

Paula recalled that up to forty people slept in one bunker. Building them took a lot of effort. "After felling trees, the men dug large holes in the ground, filled the bottom with straw and logs, stacked interlocking poles for walls, and stuffed empty spaces with tree branches." The bunkers provided both shelter and a hiding space in the event of German patrols.

In an article about her father, Yehuda Bielski's daughter described the camp and the bunkers. "The base camp—comprised of the Bielskis, their wives and girlfriends, relatives, and friends—was surrounded by smaller camps. People worked during the day and slept at night in camouflaged bunkers built underground. Everyone's skill was utilized. People improvised and endured hunger and thirst, frigid winter weather, illness, forest surgery, and personal hardships. Supplies were procured by any means possible."

As time went on and the number of refugees increased, protecting everyone became more difficult. The group mounted guards, but raids by Germans and local pro-Nazi police became more frequent in early 1943.

To better avoid detection, in July 1943, Tuvia Bielski decided to move the group about thirty miles east to a more swampy, remote area farther from settled villages. Noted one historian, "In a desperate rescue attempt, the Bielski brothers led the approximately 800 members through miles of swamps to an isolated island, called Krasnaya Gorka, in the center of the forest."

Paula and her family almost didn't make it.

A group of partisans from various fighting units including the Bielski group and escapees from the Mir ghetto on guard duty in the Naliboki Forest.

WE WADED DEEPER AND DEEPER

"Tuvia repeatedly warned the children that silence was indispensable to our survival. If we made too much noise the Nazis would follow us. I rubbed my finger over my lips, gluing them with imaginary paste," Paula wrote later.

Paula worried that Isaac might cry, but more often than not, her little brother simply fell asleep on his father's shoulders. "We waded deeper and deeper into the swamp. The cold water reached my neck. I couldn't stop shivering. Papa kissed my forehead and tried to warm my chattering teeth with stories. I dragged one exhausted foot in front of the other but I never seemed to move. The water pinned my legs in murky chains."

Whenever Paula wanted to give up, her father urged her on. "'Keep going,' he pleaded. 'Keep going.'"

At one point, they reached dry land and collapsed into sleep. When Paula awoke, the rest of the group was nowhere in sight. Panicked, she cried out, demanding to know where everyone was. "'We are lost, Papa. We are dead.'"

They were not dead, but they were lost. However, Tuvia Bielski didn't desert them. He sent a search party back to find the devoted father and his children.

Paula and her family were lucky, but they weren't out of danger yet. Their new location offered more protection from Nazi patrols, but there was little to eat; malnutrition and starvation threatened everyone. After several weeks, they had to return to the old location closer to farms and villages where they could mount raids for food around the countryside.

As the war began to turn against Hitler, the threat of German patrols eased. Back in the original camp, Paula remembered the last months of her time in the forest as peaceful. "We had a school for teaching trades, keeping men occupied, an infirmary, a soap factory, metal workshop, bakery, and bathhouse. I played games around the buildings, always with Isaac in tow."

Sonia Dzienciolski in a field of wildflowers in 1948. Like Paula and her brother, she survived thanks to the Bielski Partisans, living in the forest between the ages of five and eight.

In July of 1944, Soviet soldiers liberated the area from German occupation. It was time to leave the forest. Tuvia Bielski made a final speech. On the last day, the group blew up the camp. The Bielski leader who had helped to keep the community together proclaimed, "'Before we start a new life,' he said, 'we have to destroy the old one.'"

Then it was time to say goodbye. "Tuvia Bielski strode through the debris and hugged my father with his powerful arms. Drops of rain began falling like

Sonia Dzienciolski (bottom right) is among the children gathered around an American soldier at a displaced persons camp after leaving the forest.

tears. 'Goodbye, my dear friend,' he said. 'Take care of these darling children.'"

Paula didn't think she would ever see him again.

In 1949, when Paula was fourteen, the family, including her stepmother, Chana, whom her father had met in the forest, and half sister, Fay, immigrated to the United States. Her father opened a butcher shop in Chicago. He died in 1975.

Her brother, Isaac Koll, is a father and grandfather whose wonderful voice led him to serve as a chazzan, or cantor, leading music services at his synagogue. He remembers his sister as a skinny girl who wore braids. He also relied on Paula to protect him in the forest: Paula kept her promise to her mother.

Members of the Bielski partisan group stand by the site of a mass grave of murdered Jews shortly after liberation.

After coming to the United States, Paula became an artist, mother, and grandmother. She and her husband, Sam, live in Denver and have nine grandchildren.

Paula has often spoken to students and community groups about her experiences and has been a longtime volunteer for the Eyewitness to History Holocaust education program at the Mizel Museum in Denver, Colorado. Her memoir, *Paula's Window*, was published in 2014.

Paula did meet Tuvia Bielski one last time when he visited her father in Chicago. She told him, "'Thank you for saving my life.'"

Tuvia Bielski, who died in 1987 in New York, is credited with leading one of the most successful partisan groups of the war and creating a functioning Jewish

Group portrait of former Bielski Partisans in Israel in 1948 includes brothers Tuvia and Zus and their cousin Yehuda Bielski. Yehuda Bielski is standing on the far right. His wife, Lola, holding their daughter Nili, is seated on the far right. Tuvia Bielski is standing second from the left holding his daughter Ruth, and Zus Bielski is standing in the back center. Eli Hudes (Lola's brother) is standing between Tuvia and Zus.

community in the forest despite the cold and desperate conditions.

He is often quoted as saying, "'Don't rush to fight and die. So few of us are left, we need to save lives. It is more important to save Jews than to kill Germans.'"

Paula also recalled him saying, "'I'll be famous after I'm dead.'" And he was right. Tuvia Bielski has been the subject of books and documentaries; he was portrayed by the actor Daniel Craig in the 2008 film *Defiance*.

LOOK, LISTEN, REMEMBER: Read more about the Bielski Partisans in the USHMM Holocaust Encyclopedia: https://encyclopedia.ushmm.org/content /en/article/the-bielski-partisans.

Chapter Nine

BRONKA: THEY CAME WITH DOGS

TESTIMONY FROM A POLISH GHETTO

We escaped to the woods . . .

On December 12, 2005, an envelope arrived at the United States Holocaust Memorial Museum in Washington, DC. Inside was a three-page letter, written by hand, that began:

"To Whom It May Concern: Below find an account of my experiences during World War II. Sorry about the delay in reporting it.

"I, Bronka Harz Kurz, was born in Nadworna (South

Eastern part of Poland). When the Germans occupied South Eastern Poland in June 1941, we lived in Kolomyja, and I was ten years old."

Even though more than sixty years had passed, Bronka's words vividly convey what it was like when her peaceful childhood was shattered.

Like Paula Burger, Bronka and her family in Kolomyja (also spelled Kolomyia) had come under the control of the Soviet Union in September of 1939. Subsequently, her town, located about 170 miles east of where Paula Burger lived, was taken over by Nazi Germany in 1941. Today Kolomyja is part of Ukraine.

When the Nazis appeared, things changed at once. "Shortly after their arrival, the Germans gathered [Jewish] men and boys, ordering them to run through the streets, while the Germans in collaboration with Ukrainians hit them with nightsticks [wooden clubs].

"My brother (14 years old) was included in the raids," wrote Bronka. "A Ukrainian wanted to hit him with a rifle butt; my mother attempted to prevent it, and she was hit. A German attempted to hit me with a nightstick when I gave my father a jacket to shield him a little from being beaten. That day my brother was released but my father was arrested and beaten unmercifully in

Judke (Yehuda) Levitt hides supplies in a well in the Kovno ghetto in 1942. Jews in Kovno, the largest city in Lithuania, suffered horrendously after the Germans invaded in June of 1941. Thousands of people were killed in massacres or deported to killing centers. Despite desperately hard conditions, Jews in Kovno tried to fight back. Several sympathetic members of the local police helped arm about three hundred young people and smuggled them out of the ghetto to the Rudninkai Forest to join partisans there.

The Jewish population of Kovno also managed to leave evidence behind, including photographs, drawings, and journals. George Kadish hid a stash of photographs that survived, in part, thanks to the cooperation of Yehuda Zupowitz, a Jewish police officer in the ghetto who was tortured and killed but never revealed the location of the secret photographs.

prison. My mother bribed a Ukrainian guard, and my father escaped."

Restrictions against Jews followed. Bronka said, "Thereafter we were ordered to wear the Star of David on our arm and live in the ghetto. In the ghetto numerous people died from starvation, only people who worked outside the ghetto could get food there. Some, like my parents, risked their lives to smuggle food for their children."

Daily life in the Kolomyia ghetto was terrifying; Bronka and her family lived in constant fear. "Intermittently the Germans made raids, they came with dogs to gather people and kill them," she recalled.

Once, they heard rumors that women and children would be killed during an upcoming registration, a time when people were ordered to gather and provide their names and addresses to authorities. To avoid the registration, Bronka, now eleven, escaped with her mother, aunt, and four-year-old cousin to a forest outside a nearby village.

They evaded capture for a few days, eating berries to survive. They were arrested one night while trying to get food. Bronka's mother bribed a guard to let them go back to the ghetto, rather than being held in prison awaiting deportation.

Bronka and her mother returned to the heartbreaking news that "all the people at the registration were transported to Belzec extermination camp where they were gassed." The victims included Bronka's father, brother, and uncle. (Belzec was used both as a concentration camp and a death camp during the war.)

"Finally, it became apparent to my mother and aunt that the Germans' intention was to kill all Jews," said Bronka.

Bronka's memories are borne out by historians. According to the POLIN Museum of the History of Polish Jews in Warsaw, "In March 1942, Germans created three ghettos in the area, where they placed almost 18,000 Jews from Kolomyia and its surrounding areas. In April 1942, about 5,000, and in September 1942—almost 7,000 people were sent to the German Nazi extermination camp in Belzec. On 20 January 1943, 2,000 surviving Jews were gathered in several houses, and shot on 2 February 1943. In August 1944, when the Soviet Army entered the town, only a few Jews remained there."

Facing certain death, Bronka's mother and aunt determined to try again. "They decided to get false documents, and live as Christians in another town." Bronka's aunt and cousin made another escape attempt, which succeeded. Bronka and her mom weren't as lucky. They got out of the ghetto, but when they tried to leave the city by train, a guard at the station recognized Bronka's mother.

Bronka never forgot the terror she felt at that moment. "I begged my mother to tell me how I could kill myself to avoid tortures [sic] prior to death (I was eleven years old)."

Bronka and her mother might have been shot or put in prison. "Miraculously we were returned to the ghetto, because the Germans were planning to liquidate all the people in the ghetto within a very short time," said Bronka. "The following day at dusk we attempted our escape again, and this time we were successful."

They fled to a town where they tried to pass as Christians, living in constant fear of being recognized or stopped by soldiers. "We were frequently homeless, and didn't have enough food," said Bronka. Her aunt was caught and put in prison, leaving her child with Bronka and her mom.

Somehow, Bronka and her mother hung on. "Finally in 1944 we were liberated by the Russians, and my aunt escaped from prison. I was thirteen years old at that time."

Bronka's letter ends there. After the war, she came to the United States and married Ludwik Kurz. The couple had two children and several grandchildren. Bronka died in 2015; her husband, a professor of electrical engineering, passed away in 2017.

In noting Bronka's passing, the Columbia University School of Social Work lists Bronka as a 1956 graduate who went on to receive her PhD in 1972. Bronka and her husband each requested that memorial donations be made to a Jewish food pantry.

LOOK, LISTEN, REMEMBER: History comes alive through primary sources—letters, photographs, or simple objects that help connect us to others and imagine what their lives were like. You can see images of Bronka's handwritten letter by viewing the Bronka Harz Kurz Memoir at the USHMM: https://collections.ushmm.org /search/catalog/irn517749#?rsc=146991&cv=0&xywh= -932%2C-245%2C5278%2C4895&c=0&m=0&s=0.

Chapter Ten
WLODKA: A HIGH BRICK WALL

THE WARSAW GHETTO—PART ONE

These bits of paper would not save us for long.

I n August of 1939, seven-year-old Wlodka Blit was in the Polish mountains for a summer holiday with her parents and twin sister, Nelly. Rumors of war were everywhere, and the family rushed back to Warsaw. Within days, their world was turned upside down: German soldiers marched in and Poland soon fell to the Nazis.

Wlodka and Nelly were born on October 12, 1931, the same year as Bronka Harz Kurz. They grew up in Warsaw, long the capital of Poland, and still its largest

Polish civilians dig an anti-tank trench along a street in Warsaw, Poland, to slow the advance of the German army in September 1939. The picture was taken by American photographer Julien Bryan, who was caught in Warsaw as the invasion began and stayed for two weeks to document the first events of World War II.

city today. The twins' parents were active politically. Fearing they would both be targeted, they fled east, toward Russia, leaving Wlodka and Nelly with relatives.

There was no safety in that direction, however. Just sixteen days after Germany invaded Poland from the west, the Soviet Union invaded it from the east. (The two countries split Poland until the summer of 1941,

when Germany launched a surprise attack on the Soviet Union, bringing the entire country under Nazi domination.)

Wlodka's father, Lucjan Blit (1904–1978), was a prominent Jewish author and journalist. He was a member of a Polish Jewish socialist movement called the Bund, the German word for *federation*. Mr. Blit was captured and spent time in a Russian labor camp. Eventually, he was released and got to London in 1943.

Wlodka and Nelly's mother, Fela Herclich Blit,

smuggled herself back into Warsaw to be with her daughters. In Warsaw, the Nazis began persecuting Jews almost immediately. On October 12, 1940, Jews were forced into one area of the city, the Warsaw ghetto. The area was sealed off by a ten-foot wall the following November.

"A high brick wall topped with barbed wire was constructed around a quarter of Warsaw which became the Ghetto. We had to move there," Wlodka recalled. "My mother's family, my grandparents, aunts and uncles and two cousins, already lived in that part of Warsaw, and we moved in with them. My father's parents found a room in another part of the Ghetto."

Although her maternal grandparents' apartment was large, everyone crammed into one room because of the cold and lack of fuel. In fact, according to the USHMM, the crowded conditions meant there were about seven people to one room throughout the ghetto.

The Warsaw ghetto was the largest of at least a thousand ghettos established by the Nazis in Poland and the Soviet Union. More than 400,000 people from the city of Warsaw and surrounding communities were forced into an area of about one and a third square miles. Children and adults suffered from malnutrition, starvation, and epidemics.

"Conditions in the Ghetto were appalling— random shootings, beatings, hostage-taking, typhus, overcrowding, homelessness, people dead from hunger in the streets," Wlodka said. "Hungry children used to snatch parcels from passers-by and immediately stuff the contents in their mouths, hoping that it was food.

"But there were also secret self-help committees, secret schools, secret libraries, synagogues and clandestine political organizations. My mother was in charge of one of the few soup kitchens for starving children."

There was more to fear. "Then posters appeared in the Ghetto announcing the evacuation of everyone to 'work camps' somewhere in the east, with only those who were working for the Germans being exempted," said Wlodka. "We soon knew that these were in reality extermination camps."

Wlodka's mother was dedicated to helping children. Her job was supported by the Jewish Council, which tried to provide social services and aid to ghetto residents under nearly impossible conditions. Working for the council gave Mrs. Blit and her young daughters an exemption from being deported—for a time, at least. "But as we watched our neighbors being taken away, some quietly, some struggling, we understood these bits of paper would not save us for long," said Wlodka.

Wlodka remembered hearing soldiers in the courtyard shouting for people to assemble or be shot. "My family built a bunker in the cellar with a hidden entry,

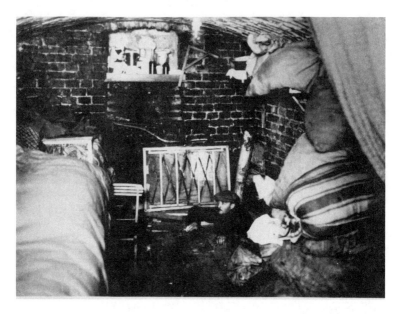

A Jewish man emerges from his hiding place below the floor of a bunker prepared for the Warsaw ghetto uprising, which took place between April 19 and May 16, 1943.

and we used to run there and hide when the raids began."

Wlodka's paternal grandparents and aunt were taken away. By the spring of 1943, Wlodka's mother realized time was running out. Unwilling to abandon her own post, she used her connections with the Bund underground to arrange escape and hiding for her girls. Her contact was engineer and underground activist Michal (sometimes spelled Michael) Klepfisz. He arranged for the Dubiels, a Polish Catholic couple living just outside the ghetto walls, to hide Wlodka and Nelly.

"The decision that we should leave the Ghetto was

taken so quickly that I cannot remember saying good-bye properly to my family," said Wlodka.

"At night we were smuggled out of the Ghetto, climbing a ladder over the Ghetto wall," she went on. Police and guards had been bribed. "We were dressed in double clothes and told that we now had new documents and new names and were never to mention to anyone who we really were."

VLADKA MEED, UNDERGROUND HEROINE

In addition to Michal Klepfisz, a young woman named Vladka Meed helped the girls survive in hiding. Born in Warsaw in 1921, Vladka had escaped the ghetto and was passing as a young Polish seamstress on the Aryan side of the wall. (We'll learn more about Vladka in the next chapter.)

Vladka's work for the resistance included rescuing children and helping to keep them safe. She was also engaged in smuggling weapons into the ghetto for Jews to mount an armed uprising. Both tasks were dangerous and difficult.

In her postwar memoir, Vladka wrote about Wlodka and Nelly. "Mrs. Dubiel, a kindly old Pole, had been somewhat disappointed; she had expected children with Aryan features, not brown eyes and dark hair. Nevertheless, she took them in." It helped that the girls spoke fluent Polish.

"Both girls were greatly distressed at being separated from their mother. They stopped eating, would not speak to anyone and hid in corners. But though they sulked in the presence of strangers, they perked up whenever I appeared. They hoped that I would have messages or letters for them [from their mother]," Vladka recalled.

THE WINDOW AND THE WALL

During one visit from Vladka, the twins pulled her to a window in the Dubiel house, which overlooked the ghetto wall. Excitedly they told her the woman they could see walking up and down on the other side was their mother. Vladka wondered how Mrs. Blit had known exactly where her daughters were hidden.

It turned out that Mr. Dubiel sometimes worked in the ghetto. The twins had begged him to find their mother and take her some food. He did, and while there, he pointed out to her the windows of his house on Wolowa Street, where her daughters were in hiding.

"Thereafter she had haunted Wolowa Street every day, and making sure she was not being watched, she would walk slowly up and down, looking up intently at the closed windows of Dubiel's house," said Vladka. "The little girls would wait for her and peep through the curtained windows."

The twins also told Vladka that if there was no sentry nearby, they sometimes tried to call out and talk to their mom. Vladka was appalled. Any passerby might report it to the Germans, endangering not only the girls' mother, but the twins and the family hiding them. The Germans, Vladka knew, didn't like anyone on the Aryan side getting close to the wall. Even gazing through a window could rouse their suspicions. She explained the dangers to Wlodka and Nelly and warned them not to do this again.

"The girls accepted my warning in silence and without objections, but their dark eyes looked at me in sorrow," Vladka remembered. "I bowed my head with a sense of guilt; why did I have to be the one to cut off the only source of joy left to these children and their mother?"

Wlodka wasn't able to stay with the Dubiels much longer—or catch heartbreakingly brief glimpses of her mom on the other side of the wall.

In the spring of 1943, just weeks after their escape, the Warsaw ghetto erupted.

Jews captured during the suppression of the Warsaw ghetto uprising in the spring of 1943 are marched to the Umschlagplatz for deportation. Of the family in the foreground, only the man survived.

Chapter Eleven
VLADKA: RESISTANCE AT ANY COST

THE WARSAW GHETTO—PART TWO

Weapons, give us weapons!

Vladka Meed was a lifeline to Wlodka and Nelly Blit. Yet keeping children safe in hiding was only part of the dangerous work she undertook for the resistance. "The goal for which we endured constant danger, hid like frightened animals, assumed false identities, moved from dwelling to dwelling to escape detection as Jews—was to obtain arms for the resistance in the ghetto."

Vladka was born Feigele Peltel on December 29, 1921, and was seventeen when war came to Poland. Vladka

Jews captured by the SS during the suppression of the Warsaw ghetto uprising march to the Umschlagplatz for deportation. This picture, probably shot in haste from a nearby window, is among a group of photos taken clandestinely by a Polish firefighter named Leszek Grzywaczewski.

lived in an apartment in the Warsaw ghetto three houses away from her widowed mother and younger brother and sister. She'd moved after the authorities came looking for her, suspicious of her involvement in underground activities. Fortunately, Vladka hadn't been home at the time.

Vladka and her family had already endured many months of hardship, never knowing what lay ahead or how long they could survive the terrible conditions. Then, in the summer of 1942, rumors about impending mass deportations became more frequent. The rumors turned out to be true.

THE DEPORTATIONS BEGIN

"Warsaw, July 22, 1942.— It is dawn. From all over the house . . . come sounds of doors opening and closing, of hurried footsteps on the stairs," wrote Vladka. "Already, in the courtyard, there is a great stir as tenants mill about anxiously asking one another, 'What is the news?'"

Fearful, Vladka left her apartment and made her way to her mother's house. While she was there, a friend burst in, saying posters had just gone up on the walls of buildings. Vladka ran back outside, jostling her way to the front so she could see the announcement.

"The letters leaped and danced before my eyes, as if to elude comprehension, but they burned themselves into my consciousness," Vladka said. This is what she read:

"'By order of the German authorities, all the Jews of Warsaw, regardless of age or sex, will be deported. Only those employed in the German workshops, the *Judrenrat* [Jewish Council], the Jewish police and the Jewish hospital will be exempt. Every deportee will be permitted to carry fifteen kilograms of luggage, including cash, valuables, and provisions for three days. Those failing to comply with this edict will be liable to the death penalty.

(Signed) The *Judenrat*'"

Vladka was surrounded by frightened and bewildered neighbors, who, like her, felt a new sense of panic. Some people may have still believed deportations meant being sent away to another location to do work. But through her contacts with the underground, Vladka was deeply suspicious of the Nazis' intentions. She'd already heard about a chilling secret report from a witness who claimed Nazis were gassing Jews to death.

The information had come from an eyewitness. A few months earlier, in February of 1942, a man named Szlama Ber Winer had made his way back to the Warsaw ghetto after escaping from Chelmno, the first of the Nazi extermination camps. Winer, who'd been forced to work as a gravedigger there, reported that innocent people were being gassed to death.

Winer shared his story with a secret group in the Warsaw ghetto called Oneg Shabbat, who were dedicated to documenting the history unfolding around them. (*Oneg Shabbat* means pleasure or joy of the Sabbath; members met on Saturdays.) Led by Polish historian Emanuel Ringelblum, who was later captured and executed, members of Oneg Shabbat collected letters, deportation lists, and copies of underground newsletters to chronicle the horrific events in which they were enmeshed. They buried this irreplaceable historical record in three underground caches. Incredibly, two caches were recovered after the war.

Vladka and her family were spared on that first day of mass deportations. She watched helplessly as others had their documents inspected. Those without employment cards were loaded onto a wagon. It was only when the street was empty that people rushed to gather scribbled notes thrown out from the wagon as it rumbled away.

After July 22, deportations increased at a furious pace, targeting residents of one block of apartments after another. Vladka and her family had hoped to go into hiding with a neighbor who had an extra room that could be blocked off with a cupboard. But the woman backed out of the plan, afraid that if caught, she'd be shot.

Then, one day in early August, the Germans surrounded the block where Vladka and her mother and siblings lived, demanding that everyone leave their apartments and assemble in the street. It was yet another selection, when residents would be funneled into two lines. Those with jobs were spared; everyone else would join the line of people being deported to some unspecified, unknown destination.

Vladka knew her sixteen-year-old sister, Henia, was at work in a public soup kitchen and was probably safe. She looked around desperately for her mother and brother, Chaim, a year younger than Henia, but couldn't spot them in the crowd. When it was her turn to have her papers inspected, Vladka presented a makeshift employment card she'd managed to get. The German in charge ordered her to the right.

It was enough to save her.

Vladka still couldn't find her mother and brother anywhere. Later, a neighbor spotted them with others in the Umschlagplatz, the loading yard and railway siding where prisoners were held before being pushed into railroad cars. Chaim managed to scribble a note in pencil, which the neighbor brought to Vladka. It was their last communication.

Vladka's mother, Hanna Peltel, and her brother, Chaim, were murdered at Treblinka, a killing center about a hundred kilometers to the northeast of Warsaw. The USHMM estimates that, in all, more than a million and a half people were killed at Treblinka; most were murdered in gas chambers as soon as they arrived.

$\sim$

It is hard to find words to describe this dark moment in history. Each death in the Holocaust was a murder robbing an innocent person of life. The mass deportations from the Warsaw ghetto were part of the unspeakably hideous "Final Solution" scheme calling for the systematic murder of Jews in the Holocaust.

The order to deport and kill the Jews of Warsaw came in July of 1942 from Heinrich Himmler, one of Hitler's top officials. According to USHMM, "Between July 22 and September 12, 1942, the German authorities deported or murdered around 300,000 Jews in the Warsaw ghetto. SS and police units deported 265,000 Jews to the Treblinka killing center and 11,580 to forced-labor camps.

"The Germans and their auxiliaries murdered more than 10,000 Jews in the Warsaw ghetto during the deportation operations. The German authorities granted only 35,000 Jews permission to remain in the ghetto, while more than 20,000 Jews remained in the ghetto in hiding. For the at least 55,000–60,000 Jews remaining in the Warsaw ghetto, deportation seemed inevitable."

The head of the Jewish Council, Adam Czerniakow, had tried to ease harsh conditions in the Warsaw ghetto by establishing food kitchens and schools. He committed suicide on July 23, 1942, the day after the deportations began. He could not bear to follow Nazi orders any longer, especially the command to deport orphaned children and send them to their deaths.

THE PROMISE OF BREAD

For Vladka and others still in the ghetto, confusion, fear, and rumors reigned. Some people tried to maintain the hope that the railroad cattle cars had taken friends and loved ones to a different town where they would find jobs waiting. Some were even lured to turn themselves in voluntarily by the promise of a ration of bread to eat in the railway car.

And still others, even those who suspected the Nazis' true intentions and had a chance to delay their deportation, refused to save themselves if it meant being separated from their children or other family members. Vladka recalled one young father who'd been forced out of hiding with his wife and baby because others in an attic feared the baby's cries would give them away. He never showed his employment card at the selection point. He stayed with the ones he loved.

"Throughout each day, while the raids continued, individuals and small groups of Jews, parents and children, trudged through the comparatively deserted streets, weighted down by bundles, baskets, and battered valises, their last pitiful belongings, towards the Umschlagplatz," said Vladka. "Exhausted by privation, emaciated or bloated by hunger, crushed by the incessant fear of being trapped, many simply gave up the struggle."

When Vladka heard a rumor that the soup kitchen where Henia worked was about to be raided, she rushed to see her sister. Vladka pleaded with Henia to leave and go into hiding. Henia refused: She was determined to stay at her post and feed others. Besides, she felt sure the kitchen crew would be spared.

Henia was wrong. She, too, was taken away.

Vladka's last link to family was gone. "I was alone now—my mother, brother and sister had gone to some dreadful unknown. My heart no longer jumped as much during a roundup as it had before. There was very little left to fear now."

Vladka made herself go on. She'd gotten a job that exempted her from selection—for a time at least. She labored from one long day to the next, sewing German military uniforms in a small shop. Whenever she and the other workers didn't make their quotas, the overseer ordered them out of line for a soup ration and sent them back to their sewing machines.

Although these workers were safe for the time being, there were still frequent searches and crackdowns. Two young mothers who worked with Vladka hid their children in a closet in the shop. The children barely escaped being discovered when soldiers stormed in, overturning piles of cloth and searching under worktables for anyone being hidden.

A SECRET MEETING

One night in October of 1942, Vladka joined a secret meeting to plan direct action against the Germans. Months before, she'd been part of a group of young activists belonging to the Bund, a Jewish socialist party, but meetings had grown rare during the height of the raids.

The Bund was among several Jewish underground organizations that worked together. One, formed in late July in response to the deportations, was an armed self-defense unit called ŻOB (Żydowksa Organizacja Bojowa), also known as the Jewish Fighting (or Combat) Organization; another was ŻZW (Żydowski Zwiazek Wojskowy), the Jewish Military Union.

Their accomplishments in the Warsaw ghetto uprising are legendary, especially compared to their size. The USHHM estimates ŻOB, led by activist Mordecai (sometimes spelled Mordechai) Anielewicz (1919–1943), had only about five hundred fighters when the uprising began, while ŻZW had half that. (More on the Warsaw ghetto uprising in the next chapter.)

Vladka listened intently at the meeting. At the end of the evening, a leader named Abrasha Blum drew her aside with a surprising request. Since Vladka spoke fluent Polish and had features that appeared Aryan—light hair and gray-green eyes—she could pass as a non-Jew.

Abrasha Blum wanted to know whether Vladka would consider sneaking out of the Warsaw ghetto to work for the Jewish resistance by posing as a Polish woman on the Aryan side. It would be extremely dangerous but Vladka willingly agreed. A few weeks later, Michal Klepfisz (who'd helped Wlodka and Nelly Blit escape) knocked on her door. Michal told Vladka that arrangements were in place on the Polish side and she should make her escape attempt in two days. The news made her head spin with excitement.

"But escape was easier said than done. For one thing, in order to slip across the wall one had to pay an exorbitant sum to the Gentile [non-Jewish] smugglers," said Vladka. "Moreover, while one might bribe the German sentinel, one could never be certain that he might not decide to shoot his victim after all. To walk out with a Jewish labor brigade on the way to an outside work assignment was the only available alternative—but a most dangerous one."

But that is exactly what she did. On December 5, 1942, just weeks before her twenty-first birthday, Vladka searched until she found a work leader to bribe. He let her join his group of laborers. Vladka was the only woman. The man told the guard she was employed in a factory kitchen but the German guard was suspicious and ordered Vladka to step into a wooden shack for further inspection.

"My blood ran cold," remembered Vladka. For in her shoes she had something dangerous: a description and map of the killing center at Treblinka. This evidence of the Final Solution had been gathered by a man named Elie Linder, who'd been deported there with his wife and child. He'd escaped by hiding under a pile of clothes and sneaking into a train car. When the train headed back for Warsaw, he'd jumped out in the darkness and made his way back.

Vladka became ever more anxious as the guard subjected her to a thorough search, pulling off her coat and even her dress, searching the pockets and inside the hem. He demanded she remove her shoes, threatening her with a whip. Vladka started unlacing them as slowly as she could.

"At that moment, as if miraculously, the door flew open, and someone shouted, '*Herr Leutnant* [Lieutenant], please come at once! A Jew has just escaped!'

"The officer dashed out, slamming the door behind him. Left alone, I dressed hurriedly and walked through the door.

"'Where are you going?' a guard stopped me.

"'To the labor battalion,' I replied, trying to sound casual. 'I have already passed inspection.'"

And Vladka walked out of the ghetto gate.

SURVIVAL ON THE OUTSIDE

It was no simple matter to masquerade as a non-Jew outside the ghetto wall. Vladka had to depend on connections and bribes. Thanks to Michal Klepfisz, she was able to obtain excellent false identity papers, essential for passing as a non-Jewish Polish citizen. Vladka's first passport was in the name of Wladslawa Kowalska. She took the code name and nickname Vladka from it, and kept the name Vladka all her life.

Vladka would assume other identities during the war, including the alias of Stanislawa Wachalska, the deceased daughter of Anna Wachalska, a non-Jewish

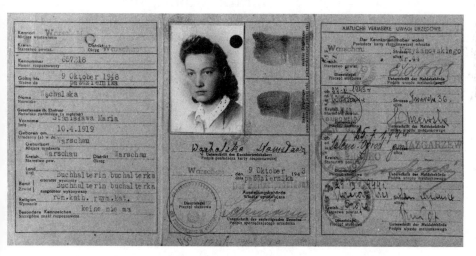

False identification card issued in name of Stanislawa Wachalska, that was used by Feigele Peltel (now Vladka Meed) while serving as a courier for the Jewish underground in Warsaw in October of 1943. The identity of Stanislawa was made possible by her mother, Anna, who was Vladka's protector and friend.

Feigele Peltel (Vladka Meed), a courier for the Jewish underground on the Aryan side of Warsaw, poses in Theater Square (Plac Teatralny) sometime in 1944.

Polish woman who became Vladka's protector and friend.

Vladka's fluent Polish was an asset. Some Jews in Warsaw had grown up speaking Yiddish, which made it impossible for them to pass as Poles. Vladka was also lucky enough to find a place to stay in the cellar of a rooming house where the landlord knew she was Jewish. Through a non-Jewish friend of Michal Klepfisz, she got a job as a seamstress with a woman who knew her true identity. "As a result, I had a refuge during the day, was earning my keep, and was provided with an identity card."

Still, danger lurked everywhere. Once, Vladka was followed and cornered by three men who tried to blackmail her, demanding payment or they would turn her in because they suspected she was Jewish. A crowd gathered around her. Vladka kept her cool and called their bluff. When they threatened to take her to the Germans she retorted, "'Very well, let's go . . . You will be called to account for casting suspicion on me and for your attempts to blackmail me.'"

Vladka walked away. The men followed her for a while but she was careful not to show any fear. When they were out of sight, she got on a trolley and took evasive tactics to make sure no one was on her tail.

Once Vladka had the basics of survival down, her next challenge was to get her assignment as a courier, or messenger. Jewish resistance fighters in the ghetto were in touch with the Polish underground, which had secret stockpiles of weapons. Vladka was briefed in a Polish convent that had a small café open to the public.

At this meeting with Leon Feiner, a Jewish Bund leader, Vladka learned the goals of the movement: to get more Polish volunteers willing to hide women and children; assist Jews already in hiding; and smuggle in money and news to leaders like Abrasha Blum in the ghetto. Most crucial of all was to find and smuggle in guns to those trapped behind the ghetto walls who were at the mercy of well-armed and ruthless captors.

After that first meeting, she reflected, "I started a new life." Along with helping children in hiding like Wlodka and Nelly Blit, Vladka now tried to procure weapons for a daring plan: an armed uprising within the ghetto.

Her first success was buying a gun from a Polish contact. She was able to smuggle the weapon into the ghetto at night through a hole in the wall. At other times, the resistance fighters bribed guards who patrolled the ghetto walls. The work was dangerous: Trusting the wrong person could mean death and betrayal.

In January of 1943, some people being deported from the ghetto turned on the German troopers before escaping into hiding places. But their ability to fight back was limited. The groups planning armed resistance, led by ŻOB, the Jewish Fighting Organization, were racing against time. There were rumors that soon all Jews would be rounded up and the ghetto destroyed.

"Very little could be accomplished with the few revolvers the organization possessed. 'Weapons, give us weapons!' was the impassioned plea of the ghetto," said Vladka.

Vladka and the others did their best to support ŻOB, smuggling in grenades, revolvers, and rifles to ŻOB fighters preparing to resist on the other side of the ghetto walls. As Vladka and the others frantically tried to find more outside help among Polish underground contacts, Michal Klepfisz had another idea: to make their own explosives.

Michal bought a chemistry book and started to use

his engineering background to experiment. Now, in addition to weapons, Vladka worked to acquire the chemicals and supplies required to make homemade explosive devices.

"It was difficult to get the gasoline, acid, and potash we needed," she wrote later. "In order not to attract attention, we purchased the 'merchandise' from suppliers in various parts of the city, and occasionally had to run the risk of transporting the ingredients across Warsaw by horse-cart. If we were discovered, it would mean death. Until they could be smuggled into the ghetto, the bags and boxes of chemicals were hidden under our own beds."

Michal's landlord arranged for him to test out his first homemade bottle bomb in a deserted factory. It worked. A Polish underground officer gave Michal more training in explosives and soon Michal was able to sneak back into the ghetto to train ŻOB fighters to make grenades and mix "Molotov cocktails," bottles filled with flammable liquid sometimes called gasoline bombs or poor man's grenades. Soon small munitions plants were set up in deserted ghetto buildings, right "under the noses of the Germans."

"The early spring of 1943 was spent in final preparations for the ghetto uprising. We now lived under constant pressure in a frenzy of activity . . ." said Vladka as she and the others stepped up their efforts to help the ŻOB.

"All of us sensed the final, decisive moment was at hand."

BENJAMIN

Another of Vladka's Jewish underground contacts was Benjamin Miedzyrzecki, who had managed to free his parents and younger sister from the ghetto. The family lived in hiding with a watchman on the grounds of a Polish cemetery.

In the difficult weeks and months to come, Vladka came to rely on his friendship—and eventually love. (Vladka and Benjamin, who simplified their last name to Meed after arriving in America after the war, were married for more than sixty years.)

Vladka Meed's future husband, Benjamin Miedzyrzecki (later Meed), in 1943. Benjamin was a member of the Jewish underground living in hiding with false papers on the Aryan side of the Warsaw ghetto wall.

STRANDED ON THE WALL

One April morning at dawn, Vladka prepared to sneak into the ghetto carrying some butter. Only that wasn't what her package actually contained. Wrapped in greasy paper, made to look like butter, Vladka was smuggling sticks of dynamite.

Clambering up a small ladder, Vladka scanned the ghetto side for her contacts. No one was in sight. Suddenly, she heard shots in the distance. Below her, someone snatched the ladder away. She was stranded. "I couldn't jump because then the 'butter' would have exploded, and there was no one to help me down. The shooting came closer," Vladka said. "There was not a soul in sight; the smugglers on both sides of the wall had disappeared. I was left, helpless, exposed on top of the wall."

Just as she was about to leap anyway, Vladka heard someone call her name. Her contact from the ghetto, Yurek (sometimes spelled Jurek) Blones, had come to help her down. They dashed into an empty building to hide in the attic from the German soldiers racing toward them. Miraculously, they weren't discovered under a heap of feathers and bedsheets.

Later, as she walked along ghetto streets on her way to deliver the dynamite, Vladka met old friends. One woman, not part of the resistance, asked her about getting a revolver to take into a hiding place. Vladka realized the mood had changed. "Jews now would resist deportation, go into hiding, defend themselves—at any cost."

Vladka delivered the dynamite to Abrasha Blum. On her next visit, he promised, he'd show her some new bunkers where he and others planned to hide from the Nazis. A roundup of all Jews was expected at any moment. Vladka returned to the other side. There would be no next visit for her.

Chapter Twelve

VLADKA AND BENJAMIN: THE SKY WAS RED

THE WARSAW GHETTO— PART THREE

The entire sky of Warsaw was red. Completely red.

Sunday evening, April 18, 1943. It was the eve of Passover, the weeklong Jewish holiday commemorating the exodus of the Israelites from Egypt. Inside the Warsaw ghetto, the news everyone had feared and dreaded for so long arrived: Lookouts on rooftops reported more German soldiers surrounding the walls. The end seemed to be at hand. For everyone knew what the Nazis intended: to destroy everyone and the ghetto itself.

"'No one slept that night,' said ŻOB fighter Tuvia Borzykowski. "'Everybody spent the time packing the most necessary articles, linen, bedding, food and taking it down to the bunkers. The moon was full and the night was unusually bright. There was more movement in the courtyards and streets than by day.'"

The next morning, April 19, 1943, Vladka Meed heard deafening bursts of gunfire and knew immediately that this was different. The Warsaw ghetto uprising had begun.

"The ghetto was surrounded by soldiers," she remembered. On the Aryan side, streets were blocked off and patrolled by Germans on motorcycles; Vladka saw machine gun muzzles protruding from the windows of houses. Detonations made the ground tremble.

Vladka, Benjamin, and other activists gathered spontaneously in one apartment. They wanted to take whatever last supplies and weapons they could get from the Polish underground, break through the German lines, and help their friends on the other side of the wall.

While Vladka and the others waited impatiently for a response from Polish underground leaders, it became clear that inside the ghetto, a fierce battle had already begun.

⌒◯

The young ŻOB commander Mordecai Anielewicz and his fighters initially took the enemy by surprise, forcing German troops outside the wall on the first day of fighting.

Kazik was the code name of a nineteen-year-old ŻOB fighter named Simha (sometimes Simcha) Rotem. Kazik knew pistols and grenades were no match against tanks and armored vehicles, but that didn't depress him. "Finally, the time had come to settle accounts with them."

On the second day of the battle, while he stood at his observation post, an SS unit approached. His commander detonated an explosion. "I saw and I didn't believe: German soldiers screaming in panicky flight, leaving their wounded behind. I pulled out one grenade and then another and tossed them. My comrades were also shooting and firing at them. We weren't marksmen but we did hit some. The Germans took off. But they came back later, fearful, their fingers on their triggers." It's estimated that twelve Germans were killed or wounded in the first assault.

On April 22, Vladka got the devastating news. Her friend and comrade Michal Klepfisz had been killed in the battle. On April 17, his birthday, he'd insisted on being the one to smuggle in a revolver he had procured. That day was also the birthday of the two-year-old daughter he left behind.

THE SKY WAS RED

As the battle raged, Vladka felt helpless on the Aryan side of the wall. She could hear gunfire, but she couldn't help. It was hard to know what was happening. She had given up the hope of getting inside. Extra guards had now been posted: There was no way to get past them.

"On the sixth day, the gunfire subsided; the Germans withdrew their heavy artillery and mounted machine guns instead. . . . The muffled detonations of bombs and grenades in the ghetto never stopped," said Vladka. "Dense clouds of smoke streaked with red flames rose from all over the ghetto, spiraling upward, obscuring the buildings. The ghetto was on fire."

Benjamin Meed also saw the ghetto burning, the fierce flames reaching so high they covered the entire city. It was a sight he would never forget. "The entire sky of Warsaw was red. Completely red. . . . And it was very heartbreaking for me," he recalled in an interview nearly fifty years later. The Polish people around him were oblivious and heartless. He felt the urge to do something or to scream, even if meant paying with his life. But he didn't.

VLADKA AND THE TWINS

On the sixth day of the uprising, Vladka went to the Dubiels' house to check on Wlodka and Nelly Blit. She was stopped by sentries several times, but managed to make her way there, claiming that her mother lived in the house.

"Reaching the house of the Dubiels at last, I found it virtually in ruins, littered with debris and dust, windows shattered, walls riddled with bullets. The elderly Mrs. Dubiel was confused and frightened. Every once in a while her husband let some Germans in to what remained of the building to search for Jews," said Vladka.

"During the German raids, old Dubiel had barely managed to conceal the children. The girls had to be rescued—but how? I tried to get near the window, but Mrs. Dubiel held me back; it was too risky. Her husband had almost been killed the day before. No Pole could show himself at a window."

On the other side of the wall, Vladka could see scenes of horror. She witnessed a woman shot as she tried to jump from an apartment onto a mattress on the ground. The woman's child was also killed.

SS troops and police had begun to raze the ghetto on the third day. Commanded by SS Major General Jürgen Stroop, troops went building by building, routing brave and determined residents from their hiding places.

SS troops force Jews to dig out the entrance to a bunker on the twentieth day of the suppression of the Warsaw ghetto uprising. The original German caption reads: "A bunker is opened." May 8, 1943.

"Though German forces broke the organized resistance within days of the beginning of the uprising, individuals and small groups hid or fought the Germans for almost a month," notes the USHMM. "Even after the end of the uprising on May 16, 1943, individual Jews hiding among the ruins of the ghetto continued to attack the patrols of the Germans and their auxiliaries. In the end, the ghetto lay in ruins.

"Approximately 42,000 of the inhabitants who did not die in the uprising were sent to forced labor and concentration camps. Another 7,000 inhabitants were deported to the Treblinka killing center, where almost all were killed in the gas chambers upon arrival."

An SS lieutenant interrogates a young Jewish resistance fighter captured on the twenty-first day of the suppression of the Warsaw ghetto uprising, May 9, 1943.

Another 7,000 Jews were killed in the fighting. In all, German commander SS General Jürgen Stroop claimed to have killed or captured 56,000 Jews.

On May 8, the ŻOB headquarters bunker was captured and Mordecai Anielewicz was killed. Within a week, the last fighters were killed. Only a few dozen fighters escaped through the city's sewer system. One of them was Kazik, who, without false identity papers and only an extra sweater, descended into a tunnel dug by the ŻZW Jewish Military Union.

He was able to make his way to a Polish underground contact who gave him food and clothing—and a shower. The experience of standing in hot, soapy water in a bright bathroom was disconcerting. "It was hard for me to believe that, just a few hours before, I had been in another world, between the crumbling walls of the Ghetto, where everything beyond the walls seemed inaccessible."

Eventually, Kazik and a companion made their way to Vladka Meed. Vladka later wrote, "Their hollow, haunted eyes and emaciated faces reflected an inner toughness, a quality that seemed to me a mystical strength drawn from a holy, shared experience, upon which I dared not intrude with my questions."

Kazik (Simha Rotem) survived the war and moved to Israel, where he was often honored for his bravery and remained active in Holocaust education efforts. He died in 2018 at the age of ninety-four, the last surviving fighter of the Warsaw ghetto uprising.

THE DREAM OF MY LIFE

The Warsaw ghetto uprising has assumed significance beyond the revolt itself. Determined, courageous fighters made a stand and their example continues to inspire others who face insurmountable odds.

On April 23, two weeks before he was killed when the command bunker was attacked, ŻOB leader Mordecai Anielewicz wrote to a comrade on the other side of the wall. As translated by Vladka Meed, his words convey the knowledge that most of the fighters will die. But he also understood the impact the uprising would have on others.

"'Something has happened beyond our wildest dreams; the Germans had to flee from the ghetto twice. One of our units held out for forty minutes, another for over six hours,'" he wrote. He went on to share details of the fighting, closing his letter with these words: "'Keep well. Perhaps we'll see each other again . . . The dream of my life has become a reality. I have lived to see Jewish defense in the ghetto in all its greatness and splendor.'"

Mattresses and furniture lie piled next to an apartment building on Gesia Street to provide a place for the inhabitants to jump during the suppression of the Warsaw ghetto uprising. The original German caption reads: "A place that had been readied for jumping and escape."

THE SOUL OF OUR STRUGGLE

"When the fighting in the ghetto had ended, the ghetto had been reduced to desolate, smoldering ruins. The Germans were busy destroying the deserted bunkers. The Warsaw ghetto was gone," said Vladka. "We, the small group of survivors hiding out in the 'Aryan sector,' felt bereft. The ghetto had been the soul of our entire struggle, the motive for all our efforts. We had lived only for the ghetto. We had drawn strength and unity from one searing need—to take vengeance."

An SS soldier stands among ruins in the Warsaw ghetto during the suppression of the uprising.

Fear permeated even the non-Jewish population of the city as SS and Gestapo patrols threatened to shoot anyone caught helping a Jew. Vladka's Bund contact, Abrasha Blum, had managed to escape the ghetto through the sewer. The father of two, he found temporary refuge in the room where Vladka lived while others tried to find a safe hiding place.

However, he was informed on and five men appeared outside Vladka's door. The German officer went to bring a car back to arrest them, locking Vladka and Abrasha in the room. Vladka burned all her papers in the gas oven. They decided to try to escape. Abrasha went first, lowering himself out the fourth-floor window using a makeshift rope of bedsheets. The rope snapped, and he landed hard on the ground, badly hurt. Vladka was arrested. She kept repeating she was not Jewish. Abrasha claimed he didn't know Vladka and had come to see the building's landlord.

Although he was injured, Abrasha Blum never let on that he knew Vladka. He was killed without betraying her. Vladka was detained and held in a cell overnight. Desperate, Vladka sent a note to her contact, Anna Wachalska, who'd hidden Jewish children and was a true friend to Vladka, Michal Klepfisz, and others. Thanks to Anna, the police were bribed and Vladka was allowed to go free.

Anna Wachalska in 1943, when she helped Vladka Meed and other Jews in Warsaw. A non-Jew, Anna provided Vladka with the alias of her own dead daughter so Vladka could survive outside the ghetto. For her work, she was recognized by Yad Vashem as one of the Righteous Among the Nations in 1964.

Anna Wachalska's friendship went even deeper. After her own daughter died, she had arranged with her priest not to report it. Later, Vladka received new identity papers as that daughter: Stanislawa Wachalska. Anna shared with Vladka her family history so if ever Vladka was questioned, she'd be able to convince the authorities of her Aryan background.

Vladka was freed, but not free. Warsaw in the spring of 1943 after the failed uprising was a dangerous place. Vladka changed her name again and went with Mrs. Dubiel and Nelly to a village for a few weeks before returning to Warsaw to continue to help Jews in hiding. What about Wlodka, the other twin?

"The Dubiels became afraid to keep two Jewish-looking children," Wlodka said. Mrs. Dubiel kept Nelly, but Wlodka was placed with another family in Warsaw. It wasn't a comfortable situation; the only bright times for Wlodka were when Vladka came to pay for her monthly care. "I waited impatiently for her visits as I had no contact with anyone else I knew, except for occasionally meeting my sister secretly in the street," remembered Wlodka.

Over the coming months, without the need to smuggle weapons, Vladka focused on relief work, trying to keep Jews in hiding safe. Vladka estimated that a small group of volunteers was trying help as many as 12,000 people in Warsaw and the surrounding cities and towns.

The twins were fortunate. "Very few Jewish children survived," Vladka said. A coordinating committee paid for their upkeep and care. While some non-Jews demanded cash payment, others risked their lives to rescue and hide Jews.

Like Anna Wachalska, Vladka's first employer, a Polish woman named Wanda Wnorowska, was a loyal friend to the Jewish resistance. When Vladka had to stop sewing to devote herself to relief work, Wanda took on other Jews, protecting them and helping them to live on the Aryan side. Eventually, her home became a meeting place for the resistance. Another friend sold her jewelry and donated the money to rescue efforts. Had there been more people like these, Vladka reflected later, more Jews might have survived.

THE PEOPLE OF WARSAW REVOLT

Jews and non-Jews joined forces beginning on August 1, 1944, when the people of Warsaw rebelled against

Polish teenager Jan Kostanski (right); his two sisters, Jadzia and Danuta; and his divorced mother, Wladislawa, helped Jewish friends and neighbors during the German occupation of Warsaw. Jan's mother hid widower Ajzyk Wierzbicki and his family, while Jan smuggled food into the ghetto.

Here, Jan crouches with others in a bunker during the Warsaw Polish uprising, which took place from August to October of 1944 (not to be confused with the Warsaw ghetto uprising of 1943). There is romance in this story too. After the war, Jan's mother married Mr. Wierzbicki. Jan married his daughter, Nacha, and they moved to Australia. In April of 1984, Jan and Wladislawa Kostanski were recognized by Yad Vashem as Righteous Among the Nations.

their Nazi oppressors and tried to liberate their city. The uprising had been launched with hopes that Soviet troops were advancing and would intervene. It became known as the Warsaw Polish uprising to distinguish it from the 1943 revolt in the ghetto. It lasted until October of 1944, when the Germans crushed the effort and evacuated the city before completely razing it.

During this harrowing time, Vladka and Benjamin struggled to survive in underground bunkers and cellars. With the relief effort in disarray and many of their companions captured or killed, they decided to flee the city. They did not return until after it had been liberated. Soviet troops finally arrived in January of 1945. Most of Warsaw was in ruins.

Benjamin and Vladka were among the few who survived the Warsaw Polish uprising. The USHMM estimates approximately 166,000 people died in the months of fighting, including 17,000 Jews.

"When the Russian soldiers finally arrived, I thought I was the only Jew left in Poland apart from Wladka [Vladka Meed]," said Wlodka Blit.

Wlodka had been put on a train with the family that was hiding her. They managed to jump off at a village and, in the winter of 1945, walked back to the ruins of Warsaw. She only had a pair of torn sandals. Eventually, she found Mrs. Dubiel and her twin sister, Nelly.

The sisters lost both sets of grandparents, as well as aunts, uncles, and cousins. Their mother, Fela Herclich Blit, who tried to help the hungry children, was also killed. In 1946, at age fourteen, Wlodka and Nelly were able to go to London and join their father, whom they hadn't seen in six years.

In an e-mail dated January of 2019, Wlodka Blit

Robertson told me, "We went to school where I did well enough to train as a radiographer. I met my husband Bruce when we were students through the Labour Party youth section and we were married for 61 years. I have three children Isabel, Susie and Mark and five grandchildren and one great grandchild—all doing well and we are all in close touch."

When I asked her what advice she has for young people today, she said, "I would tell young people that they are the future and hopefully my story will make them want to make the world a happier and safer place for everyone."

LOOK, LISTEN, REMEMBER: Wlodka Blit Robertson continues to speak out about her experiences during the Holocaust. You can listen to Wlodka (spelled Wlodja here) in this British Library recording: https://sounds.bl.uk/Oral-history/Jewish-Holocaust-survivors/021M-C0410X0025XX-0100V0.

BRAVE JEWISH TEENS IN HUNGARY

Just as many of the fighters in the Warsaw ghetto uprising were teenagers, brave Jewish teens in Hungary risked their lived during the Holocaust. Members of the Hungarian Zionist Youth Movement took part in resistance and rescue work, providing Jews with false identity papers, warning people of planned deportations, and helping to set up more than fifty safe homes to hide children. The USHMM credits the group with saving 6,000 Jews.

The Holocaust in Hungary occurred late in the war. The Jewish community in Hungary, which was allied with Germany, remained mostly intact until the Hungarian government agreed to deportations in March of 1944. The USHMM estimates that about 440,000 Hungarian Jews were murdered at Auschwitz. The reckoning of Holocaust history in Hungary is not over. The country has seen a rise in antisemitism along with governmental policies that disavow the past.

Close-up portrait of three members of the Zionist underground in Budapest, Hungary, possibly from 1944. On the far right is David Gur. Born in 1926, he became active with the Zionist youth movement in the spring of 1944, as deportations of Hungarian Jews began. In December of 1944, he was caught in a forgery workshop. He was taken to a military prison but escaped thanks to a daring rescue operation.

David survived the war and spent twenty years compiling a record of the Hungarian underground movement. His book was published in 2004 as *Brothers for Resistance and Rescue: The Underground Zionist Movement in Hungary during World War II.*

Portrait of Vera Lefkovics (later Weisz), a member of the Hungarian Zionist youth resistance organization, about 1944. As a teen, Vera escaped an execution squad by leaping into the freezing Danube River after she was caught by the Nazis for her resistance work hiding over a hundred Jewish women and children in Budapest.

Portrait of Agnes Wertheimer (later Zahava Arieli), a member of the Hungarian Zionist youth resistance organization. Born in Slovakia, Zahava became part of the underground movement in Budapest. She delivered forged identity documents to help fellow Jews hide. She was twice captured and tortured but managed to escape and survive the war.

EPILOGUE

LIBERATION AND SORROW

Jews captured during the Warsaw ghetto uprising are marched to the Umschlagplatz for deportation in the spring of 1943. In nearly all cases, those few left behind never saw their loved ones again.

An African American soldier with the 12th Armored Division, Seventh US Army, stands guard over a group of German soldiers captured in the forest in April of 1945. Adolf Hitler committed suicide on April 30. On May 7, Germany signed official surrender papers, which went into effect the following day. May 8 is now celebrated as VE Day, or Victory in Europe Day.

On August 15, 1945, after the atomic bombings of Hiroshima and Nagasaki, the surrender of Japan was announced. Official surrender papers were signed on September 2, 1945.

It must all be recorded with not a single fact omitted. And when the time comes—as it surely will—let the world read and know what the murderers have done.

—**EMANUEL RINGELBLUM,** *historian of the Warsaw ghetto, executed in 1944*

If that evil had conquered the world . . . we wouldn't be here.
   You are all survivors.

—**LEO BRETHOLZ,** *Holocaust survivor*

VOICES OF GRIEF AND JOY

With the surrender of Germany, World War II ended in Europe on May 8, 1945. The war's end brought liberation to those who had lived under Nazi oppression for years. It also brought new horrors as the world began to understand the full scope of the Holocaust and the Nazis' insidious Final Solution.

For many, including some of the people we have followed in this book, sorrow and happiness were intertwined. Eva and Martin Deutschkron, who had achieved almost the impossible by hiding in Berlin, Germany, faced the need to rebuild their lives, while mourning the families they had lost. Sisters Chella and Flora Velt from the Netherlands had survived a horrendous ordeal, but their relief was mixed with sorrow when they realized their beloved father had been murdered. Their physical and emotional recovery would take a long time, and their dedication to Holocaust education would last a lifetime.

Alfred and Ernest Moritz were delighted to be reunited with their parents. At the same time, Alfred wrote later that their adjustment took time. The brothers had been on their own for a long time. Paula Burger and her brother, Isaac, had survived in the forest. But with the war's end came a stepmother who could never replace their own.

In this section are gathered just a few voices that capture the gamut of emotions survivors felt as the war ended.

AN OUTSTRETCHED HAND
BRUSSELS, BELGIUM

"It was night. We were roaming the streets, looking for the advancing column. Rumors of sightings were spreading like wildfire. There was sporadic shooting, but in our state of near hysteria we were paying no heed to it. In the excitement, our small band had fragmented and I was on my own without even realizing it.

"Suddenly, huge dark masses appeared. These were tanks, clearly part of the Allied vanguard. People were screaming wildly, trying to climb on the tanks to grasp the soldiers sitting on top. I joined them, frantically trying to reach the outstretched hand of a grinning soldier.

"This hand represented for me the end of years of fear and anxiety, and I felt it a matter of life or death to be able to shake it. After the release of pent-up emotions triggered by the handshake, I roamed the streets all night, with many people around me doing the same."

George Brawerman was born in 1927 and survived the Holocaust by hiding in Belgium.

Dutch citizens celebrate the liberation of the city of Utrecht in the Netherlands in May of 1945.

FOR THAT ONE DAY— AMSTERDAM, THE NETHERLANDS

"I don't know where they got the lights, but at night we had lights and boats were laid across the canals and you could walk from one side to the other over the boat. . . . And it was wonderful. It was the most wonderful, wonderful day . . . I can remember.

And I didn't think—I didn't let myself think about my parents and my [sister] for that one day. And then afterwards, I said, 'Now what? Now what?'"

> Barbara Ledermann Rodbell lived in the Netherlands. She and her family were neighbors and friends of the family of Anne and Margot Frank. Barbara went into hiding and joined the resistance. Her parents and sister were murdered in the Holocaust.

Captured German troops are marched through the streets during the liberation of Amsterdam in May of 1945.

General Dwight D. Eisenhower, Supreme Commander, Allied Expeditionary Force, led the invasion of Normandy on D-Day (June 6, 1944) and the final Allied assault to defeat Nazi Germany. Here he pays an official visit to the Netherlands after liberation in 1945.

THE ANGRESS FAMILY
AMSTERDAM, THE NETHERLANDS

"On May 8, 1945 the war was officially declared over. Having waited so anxiously for this day to come, I now found it hard to believe. It meant that I didn't need to hide anymore. It meant that I could open a door and step out on the street without fear of being arrested. Most importantly, I hoped, it meant being reunited with my family again. . . .

"Yes, World War II was finally over. I hoped that it would never be forgotten."

Fred (Fritz) P. Angress, survivor who hid during the Holocaust.

"When Mutti [mother] and I approached, Fritz [his brother Fred] was standing at the second-floor window of the pharmacy house, dressed in a suit and tie, watching the girls pass by outside. When I called him below and he saw me, he nearly fell out of the window.

"We then went back to my mother's room, where suddenly and unexpectedly our younger brother, Hans, showed up, bringing a bunch of crumpled flowers because it was Mother's Day. He was also very surprised to see me in Amsterdam so shortly after the end of the war, and as an American soldier at that."

Werner T. Angress, survivor and American soldier, who returned to Amsterdam to find his mother and two younger brothers who had survived in hiding.

THERE IS NO ONE HERE—
THE WARSAW GHETTO

"Quiet, heart! Stop racing so. There is nothing and no one to be afraid of now. Don't you see that there is no one here, that there are only desolate ruins and rubble and wreckage wherever your eyes turn? Why, then

A young girl lights Sabbath candles in an unidentified postwar OSE children's home in France, sometime between 1945 and 1950. The USHMM estimates that as many as one and a half million children, a million of them Jewish, were murdered during the Holocaust. Thousands of children and teens were orphaned or lived in displaced persons camps hoping to find surviving relatives. Others immigrated to Israel both before and after it became a state in 1948.

the fear and trembling? Remember, you have already witnessed horrible scenes here amidst roaring tongues of flame and billowing smoke . . .

A postwar drawing by Peretz Chorshati showing his unsuccessful postwar search for relatives in the Warsaw ghetto.

"True, then there was still some small spark of life; people still tried, still struggled . . . there was still a glimmer of hope . . .

"But how different this scene! It is best not to think of all that now. Perhaps it is better only to gaze in silence upon this dead and desolate wilderness, where every stone, every grain of sand is sodden with Jewish blood and tears.

"Silence . . .

"The aching eyes devour the scene; every stone, every heap of rubble is a reminder of the Holocaust. Here a protruding length of pipe, there a bent iron rail, there a charred sapling—these are what is left of our devastated world. My eyes fall upon the remains of a torn, soiled prayer book, on a rusty, dented pot, and I see my home again—my father and mother . . .

"But what of my own grief? The scene is the same in a thousand other towns, a hundred other ghettos; my sorrow repeated ten thousand times. But the figures, the incredible statistics, how do they compare, how can they express what has happened?"

Vladka Meed, Holocaust survivor and Jewish underground activist in Warsaw, Poland.

WE MUST TELL OUR STORY

It seems fitting to end this book with the reflections of the extraordinary Vladka Meed, whose life was shaped by the events that shattered her family and community when she was a teen.

Vladka and Benjamin Meed arrived in the United States in 1946. Benjamin had eight dollars in his

Buildings destroyed by the SS during the suppression of the Warsaw ghetto uprising, April 19–May 16, 1943. Today, the Umschlagplatz Monument on the corner of Stawki Street and Dzika Street in Warsaw memorializes the lives of the 300,000 innocent men, women, and children deported from this site.

Vladka Meed shakes the hand of President Jimmy Carter at a White House Rose Garden ceremony marking the official presentation of the report of the US Holocaust Commission. Also pictured are Vladka's husband, Benjamin Meed (second from the left), and Elie Wiesel (third from the left), commission chairperson, Holocaust survivor, and author who won the Nobel Peace Prize in 1986.

pocket. As they started a family (the couple had two children) and built their new lives together, the Meeds also devoted their talents and energies to Holocaust education.

They were instrumental in forming the American Gathering of Jewish Holocaust Survivors and Their Descendants, which has brought people together since 1983. They established the Benjamin and Vladka Meed Registry of Jewish Holocaust Survivors, which is now managed by USHMM. In 1984, Vladka initiated the

Holocaust and Jewish Resistance Teachers Program for high school educators teaching about the Holocaust.

In 1979, Vladka and Benjamin were members of the commission established by Jimmy Carter and chaired by Nobel Peace Prize winner Elie Wiesel. The commission was charged with submitting a report exploring the possibility of establishing and maintaining a memorial to those who perished in the Holocaust. Benjamin died in 2008 at the age of eighty-eight. Vladka passed away in 2012 at age ninety. At the time of Benjamin's death, the couple had been married more than sixty years.

The living memorial to the Holocaust was eventually realized in the United States Holocaust Memorial Museum, which opened on the National Mall in Washington, DC, in 1993. As of 2019, more than forty million people had visited the museum.

The extraordinary resources on its website have made it the world's leading authority. Nearly all the photographs in this book were donated to the USHMM by survivors and their descendants. Thousands more are available online. Like the precious letters Mina Dümig gave to Ruth David, they help to give the dead a voice.

Benjamin Meed once said, "We must tell our story to be worthy of the memory of our six million martyrs who cannot speak for themselves."

For our part, now and always, we can listen and do what we can to keep these stories alive. There must be one who remembers.

Excavating the box of negatives and documents that photographer Henryk Ross, who chronicled life under the Nazis, buried in the ghetto at 12 Jagielonska Street, Lodz, Poland, March 1945. Henryk Ross worked for the Jewish Council in the Lodz ghetto in Poland, and while he took official images, he also took risks to photograph and document the suffering of families, many of whom were deported to death camps at Chelmno and Auschwitz. Ross buried his negatives when the ghetto was liquidated in the fall of 1944. Ross survived, along with about half of his 6,000 negatives, which are still viewed today in exhibitions to tell the story of the Holocaust.

GLOSSARY

Anschluss

The annexation of Austria by Germany on March 12, 1938.

antisemitism

Hostility toward, violence against, or persecution of Jews.

Aryans

People who speak one or more of the Indo-European languages. In Nazi Germany, the term was wrongly identified as a race of blond, blue-eyed European people who were considered superior to others.

Auschwitz

A network of main concentration and extermination camps, along with satellite camps in Nazi-occupied Poland.

brownshirts

Nickname for the SA, a Nazi paramilitary group.

Bund

Jewish socialist movement active in Russia, Poland, and Lithuania. The word means *federation* in German.

fascism

Political ideas and a movement that includes a rejection of democratic values and elections; rule by a small elite; extreme militarism; and a strong, authoritarian, and controlling government.

führer

German word for leader or guide. It became a synonym for Adolf Hitler in Nazi Germany.

genocide

Deliberate slaughter of a large group of people, especially those of a certain ethnic group, nation, or religion.

Gestapo

The German state secret police, from the German *Geheime Staatspolizei*. The Gestapo fell under the administration of the SS and had the power to arrest people.

Judenraete

Jewish councils set up in the ghettos by the Germans to implement Nazi policies. Those who worked for the councils also tried to provide services to the community, and were temporarily exempt from deportation. Some members tried to use their positions to save children and others from being transported to concentration or extermination camps.

Kindertransport

Children's transports that rescued approximately 10,000 from the Nazis.

Kristallnacht

Nazi campaign of violent attacks against the Jews, November 9–10, 1938.

Nazi Party

Abbreviation of the National Socialist German Workers' Party (*Nationalsozialistische Deutsche Arbeiterpartei*).

partisan

Member of a secret armed group fighting against an occupying force.

pogrom

A Russian word meaning to demolish violently, pogrom refers to violent attacks by local non-Jewish populations on Jews.

razzia

A raid or roundup.

Roma

A name for Roma or Romani people, who often lead an itinerant lifestyle.

SA

Abbreviation of *Sturmabteilung*, or assault division, a Nazi paramilitary group also known as storm troopers or brownshirts. Members of the SA were responsible for many atrocities against Jews.

Shoah

Hebrew word for the Holocaust.

SS

Abbreviation of *Schutzstaffel*, a Nazi paramilitary organization.

Wannsee Conference

A meeting of senior Nazi officials and the SS on January 20, 1942, which outlined plans for the Final Solution, the roundup and deportation of innocent Jewish men, women, and children to extermination camps in Nazi-occupied Poland.

ŻOB

Abbreviation of *Żydowska Organizacja Bojowa*, translated as Jewish Fighting (or Combat) Organization, which led the Warsaw ghetto uprising in the spring of 1943.

SELECTED TIMELINE OF WORLD WAR II IN EUROPE

1918
End of WWI. The war pitted Germany and Austria-Hungary against Britain, France, Russia, and the United States.

1919
The Treaty of Versailles ends WWI and imposes harsh economic conditions on Germany.

1925
Austrian-born WWI veteran Adolf Hitler fans the fires of German resentment; the first volume of his political autobiography, *Mein Kampf* ("My Struggle") blames Jews and contains harsh antisemitic rhetoric.

1933
Hitler becomes chancellor of Germany and the Nazi Party immediately begins the persecution of Jews.

1935

The Nuremberg Laws strip German Jews of their citizenship and impose other restrictions.

1938

On March 12, the Nazis annex Austria, an event known as the Anschluss. Persecution of Austrian Jews begins immediately.

On November 9–10, Jewish synagogues are burned and businesses are ransacked during Kristallnacht (Night of Broken Glass). Following the violence, many Jewish men are arrested. The British government agrees to accept refugee Jewish children. About 10,000 children escape from Germany, Austria, and Czechoslovakia in 1938 and 1939. Most are never reunited with their families.

1939

On September 1, Germany invades Poland; because of its prior commitment to protect Poland, Great Britain declares war on Germany on September 3. The outbreak of war makes immigration nearly impossible for millions of Jews in Europe.

1940

On April 9, Germany launches a surprise invasion of Denmark and Norway.

On May 10, Germany attacks the Netherlands, which surrenders on May 14. Immediately, Dutch Jews, and about 25,000 Jews who had fled Germany hoping for safety in Holland, are in danger from Nazi antisemitic actions.

Germany also invades Luxembourg, Belgium, and France.

1941

In June, Germany invades the Soviet Union, which joins the Allies. Poland comes under total Nazi occupation. On December 7, Japan attacks Pearl Harbor. The United States enters the war.

The Nazis begin adoption of the "Final Solution," the state-sponsored, systematic murder of Jews and others.

1942

At the Wannsee Conference in Germany on January 20, senior government officials ensure that all departments will cooperate and implement the Final Solution.

1944

On June 6, the Allies land on the beaches of Normandy, beginning the campaign to liberate Nazi-occupied Europe and defeat Germany.

1945

Hitler commits suicide on April 30. Germany surrenders on May 7, to take effect on May 8, which is now known as VE Day, or Victory in Europe Day.

The United States drops atomic bombs on Hiroshima (August 6) and Nagasaki (August 9). Japan surrenders on August 15 and signs formal surrender documents on September 2.

1993

On April 22, the United States Holocaust Memorial Museum is dedicated as a living monument to those who died in the Holocaust. Its first visitor, on April 26, is His Holiness the Dalai Lama of Tibet.

LOOK, LISTEN, REMEMBER: RESOURCES TO EXPLORE

A visit to the United States Holocaust Memorial Museum or a local historical society or Jewish museum can be a powerful, life-changing experience. We are also fortunate to have the ability to access many resources online. Here are some ideas for learning more about the events and people in this book. Remember that websites and their contents do change.

Today there are still people who promote racist, anti-semitic, and neo-Nazi viewpoints. As history detectives in search of facts, it's a good idea to develop careful Internet searching practices. For example, always examine the domain name of online searches and look for reliable sources. Most American museums and non-profit organizations have an extension of ".org."

Topics here are arranged in alphabetical order. A good place to begin is the United States Holocaust Memorial Museum's Holocaust Encyclopedia, where historians and experts have synthesized accurate information: https://encyclopedia.ushmm.org. From the USHMM home page (https://www.ushmm.org/) simply click on "Learn About the Holocaust." Individual articles in the Holocaust Encyclopedia that are mentioned in the text are included here, but you can search for other topics once you are online.

When in doubt, or when starting a new search, it's helpful to include the United States Holocaust Memorial Museum (USHMM) in your search term. It's the most reliable source of information about the Holocaust in the world. For instance, a Google search for "gays in the Holocaust USHMM" will bring up an article for students entitled "Persecution of Homosexuals" at https://www.ushmm.org/learn/students/learning-materials-and-resources/homosexuals-victims-of-the-nazi-era/persecution-of-homosexuals.

If you need help, check with a librarian, teacher, or parent to locate information or if these links become out-of-date. Some of the museum websites listed here are in languages other than English. Most provide an online "translate" option into English, which quite often is an icon of a flag, usually either that of the United Kingdom or the United States.

MUSEUM WEBSITES AND ONLINE RESOURCES

General informational sites are listed first,
followed by specific countries.

ANTISEMITISM

The survivors profiled in this book were brave enough to tell their stories because, in part, they wanted to encourage people to be more aware of antisemitism and speak up against discrimination. The Anti-Defamation League (ADL), an organization that protects Jewish people, has excellent resources to help prevent bullying and promote ally behavior.

Anti-Defamation League
https://www.adl.org

Bend the Arc, A Jewish Partnership for Justice
https://www.bendthearc.us/about

THE HOLOCAUST

American Gathering of Jewish Holocaust Survivors and Their Descendants
https://amgathering.org

Auschwitz Museum and Memorial
http://auschwitz.org/en

Children during the Holocaust
https://encyclopedia.ushmm.org/content/en/article
/children-during-the-holocaust

Genocide of Roma People
https://encyclopedia.ushmm.org/content/en/article
/genocide-of-european-roma-gypsies-1939-1945

The Holocaust Explained: Auschwitz-Birkenau
The Wiener Library for the Study of the Holocaust and
Genocide
https://www.theholocaustexplained.org/the-final-solution
/auschwitz-birkenau/kanada-kommando

Jewish Badge during the Nazi Era
https://encyclopedia.ushmm.org/content/en/article
/jewish-badge-during-the-nazi-era

Museum of Jewish Heritage
https://mjhnyc.org

The Riga Ghetto Museum
http://www.rgm.lv/visit/?lang=en

United States Holocaust Memorial Museum
https://www.ushmm.org

USHMM Benjamin and Vladka Meed Registry of
Jewish Holocaust Survivors
https://www.ushmm.org/online/hsv/source_view
.php?SourceId=1

USHMM Holocaust Encyclopedia: Documenting
Victims
https://encyclopedia.ushmm.org/content/en/article
/documenting-numbers-of-victims-of-the-holocaust
-and-nazi-persecution

USHMM Holocaust Encyclopedia: Ghettos
https://encyclopedia.ushmm.org/content/en/article
/ghettos

USHMM Holocaust Encyclopedia: Nazi Camps
https://encyclopedia.ushmm.org/content/en/article
/nazi-camps

MORE ABOUT FRANCE

BBC article on the fall of France

https://www.bbc.co.uk/history/worldwars/wwtwo/fall
_france_01.shtml

Camp Les Milles Museum

http://www.campdesmilles.org/index.html

Camp Les Milles in USHMM Holocaust Encyclopedia

https://encyclopedia.ushmm.org/content/en/article
/les-milles-camp

Château de la Hille: Read more about the rescuers
and children of Château de la Hille

https://www.ariege.com/en/discover-ariege
/occupation-and-resistance/children-château-la-hille

Children's Homes in France during the Holocaust:
online exhibition by Yad Vashem

https://www.yadvashem.org/yv/en/exhibitions/childrens
-homes/index.asp

France in the Holocaust Encyclopedia at USHMM

https://encyclopedia.ushmm.org/content/en/article/france

Jewish Virtual Library on the Vichy Regime
https://www.jewishvirtuallibrary.org
/the-french-vichy-regime#9

OSE
OSE-France
http://www.ose-france.org/categories/quisommesnous
/notre-histoire/en

Tablet Magazine article on the French Resistance
https://www.tabletmag.com/jewish-arts-and-culture
/books/201308/was-the-french-resistance-jewish

MORE ABOUT HUNGARY

USHMM Exhibition, The Holocaust in Hungary:
70 Years Later
https://www.ushmm.org/information/exhibitions
/online-exhibitions/special-focus/the-holocaust-in-hungary

USHMM Statement on Hungary
https://www.ushmm.org/information/press/press-releases
/united-states-holocaust-memorial-museum-statement
-on-hungary

Holocaust Museum in Budapest

https://www.washingtonpost.com/world/europe/hungarys
-orban-has-asked-a-rabbi-to-take-over-a-stalled-holocaust
-museum-many-jews-still-fear-a-whitewash/2019/08/25
/9f9d0e1a-b78e-11e9-8e83-4e6687e99814_story.html

MORE ABOUT THE NETHERLANDS

Beyond Anne Frank: The Dutch Tell Their Full Holocaust Story

https://www.nytimes.com/2016/07/18/world/europe
/beyond-anne-frank-the-dutch-tell-their-full-holocaust
-story.html

Daring to Resist: 3 Women Face the Holocaust

Barbara Ledermann Rodbell is featured in this film.
https://www.pbs.org/daringtoresist/barbara.html

German Invasion of the Netherlands, Anne Frank House

https://www.annefrank.org/en/anne-frank/go-in-depth
/german-invasion-netherlands

Verzets Resistance Museum

https://www.verzetsmuseum.org/museum/en/tweede
-wereldoorlog/kingdomofthenetherlands/thenetherlands
/thenetherlands-may_1943_-_may_1944/hand_in

Vught Concentration Camp
https://www.jewishvirtuallibrary.org/vught-concentration
-camp
https://encyclopedia.ushmm.org/content/en/article
/herzogenbusch-main-camp-vught

MORE ABOUT POLAND

The Bielski Brothers
https://www.yadvashem.org/articles/general/solidarity
-bielski-brothers.html

The Bielski Partisans at USHMM
https://encyclopedia.ushmm.org/content/en/article/the
-bielski-partisans

Images from the Oneg Shabbat Archive at Yad
Vashem
https://www.yadvashem.org/yv/en/exhibitions/ringel
-blum/index.asp

Kolomyia Ghetto at POLIN Museum of the History
of Polish Jews
https://sztetl.org.pl/en/towns/k/812-kolomyia/99-history
/137492-history-of-community

Nowogródek
https://www.yadvashem.org/untoldstories/database/index
.asp?cid=502

Oneg Shabbat Archive at USHMM
https://encyclopedia.ushmm.org/content/en/article
/the-oneg-shabbat-archive

Warsaw Ghetto Uprising (1943) at USHMM
Holocaust Encyclopedia
https://encyclopedia.ushmm.org/content/en/article
/warsaw-ghetto-uprising

Warsaw Polish Uprising (1944) at USHMM
https://www.ushmm.org/learn
/timeline-of-events/1942-1945/warsaw-polish-uprising

PEOPLE IN THIS BOOK: ORAL HISTORIES, ARTICLES, AND INTERVIEWS

Ruth Oppenheimer David
BBC News
https://www.bbc.com/news/av/uk-england-leicestershire
-19641062/leicester-woman-honoured-by-germany
-for-holocaust-work

Herb DeLevie
Wisconsin Historical Society
https://www.wisconsinhistory.org/HolocaustSurvivors
/DeLevie.asp

Eva Lauffer Deutschkron
Wisconsin Historical Society
https://www.wisconsinhistory.org/HolocaustSurvivors
/Deutschkron.asp

David Gur
Yad Vashem
https://www.yadvashem.org/remembrance/archive/2007
/torchlighters/gur.html

Jan Kostanski

Righteous Among the Nations

https://www.yadvashem.org/righteous/stories/konstanski
.html

Jan Kostanski's Letter about the Warsaw Ghetto

https://www.yadvashem.org/righteous/stories/konstanski
/jan-kostanski-letter.html

Chella Velt Meekcoms Kryszek

Oregon Jewish Museum and Center for
Holocaust Education

http://www.ojmche.org/oral-history-people/velt-chella

Hanne Hirsch Liebmann

USHMM

https://encyclopedia.ushmm.org/content/en/oral-history
/hanne-hirsch-liebmann-describes-a-childrens-aid-society
-ose-visit-and-life-in-le-chambon-sur-lignon

Hanne Hirsch and Max Liebmann

http://khc.qcc.cuny.edu/goodness/reflect/hanne-and-max

Benjamin Meed

Holocaust Encyclopedia, USHMM

https://encyclopedia.ushmm.org/content/en/article
/benjamin-meed

Benjamin Meed Warsaw Uprising Personal History Video

https://www.ushmm.org/exhibition/personal-history/media_oi.php?MediaId=1096

Benjamin Meed's Obituary in the *New York Times*

https://www.nytimes.com/2006/10/26/obituaries/26meed.html

Vladka Meed
Jewish Women's Archive

https://jwa.org/encyclopedia/article/meed-vladka

Vladka Meed's Obituary in the *New York Times*

https://www.nytimes.com/2012/11/25/world/vladka-meed-who-infiltrated-warsaw-ghetto-dies-at-90.html

Vladka Meed USC Shoah Foundation Oral History Interview, 1996

https://sfi.usc.edu/content/vladka-meed-0

Alfred Moritz
United States Holocaust Memorial Museum

https://collections.ushmm.org/search/catalog/irn598422

Alfred Münzer
United States Holocaust Memorial Museum
https://collections.ushmm.org/search/catalog/irn511187

Frederik Jacques Philips
https://www.nytimes.com/2005/12/07/business/frederik
-philips-dies-at-100-businessman-saved-dutch-jews.html

Gertrud Sonnenberg
United States Holocaust Memorial Museum
https://collections.ushmm.org/search/catalog/irn505503

Johan van Hulst, Dutch Rescuer
https://www.jewishvirtuallibrary.org/johan-van-hulst

BIBLIOGRAPHY

* Titles of special interest to young readers.

SPECIAL THANKS

The author is grateful to the curatorial and permissions staff who provided permissions to access materials and were unfailingly helpful in responding to inquiries. Special thanks to Michael Simonson, archivist and registrar at the Leo Baeck Institute, New York; to the staff of the United States Holocaust Memorial Museum; Penny Nisson, Director of Education at the Mizel Museum; Paul E. Hedges, Digital Collections Coordinator for Library, Archives and Museum Collections at the Wisconsin Historical Society; and to Judy Margles, Director; Anne LeVant Prahl, Curator of Collections; and Becca Biggs, Communications Manager at the Oregon Jewish Museum and Center for Holocaust Education.

Special thanks to Ruth David for permission to quote from *Child of Our Time* and *Life-Lines*; to Wlodka Robertson for permission to quote from her piece, "Surviving in Warsaw," in *We Remember*; to Dr. Jacques Semelin for use of a quote from *Resisting Genocide*, and to Paula Burger and the Mizel Museum for permission to quote from *Paula's Window*.

BOOKS

Ajzensztadt, Amnon. *Endurance: Chronicles of Jewish Resistance.* Oakville, ON: Mosaic, 1987.

Angress, Werner T. *Between Fear & Hope: Jewish Youth in the Third Reich.* Translated by Werner T. Angress and Christine Granger. New York: Columbia University Press, 1988.

———. *Witness to the Storm: A Jewish Journey from Nazi Berlin to the 82nd Airborne, 1920–1945.* Translated by Werner T. Angress with Christine Granger. Durham, NC: CreateSpace, 2012.

Baker, Leonard. *Days of Sorrow and Pain: Leo Baeck and the Berlin Jews.* New York: Oxford University Press, 1981. First published by Macmillan, 1978.

Bard, Mitchell G. *48 Hours of Kristallnacht: Night of Destruction/Dawn of the Holocaust.* Guilford, CT: The Lyons Press, 2008.

*Bartoletti, Susan Campbell. *Hitler Youth: Growing Up in Hitler's Shadow.* New York: Scholastic, 2005.

Bauman, Janina. *Winter in the Morning: A Young Girl's Life* in the Warsaw Ghetto and Beyond 1939–1945. London: Virago, 1986.

Bender, Sara, and Shmuel Krakowski, eds. *The Encyclopedia of the Righteous Among the Nations: Rescuers of Jews during the Holocaust. Poland.* Israel Gutman, Editor-in-chief. Jerusalem: Yad Vashem, 2004.

Bentwich, Norman. *They Found Refuge: An Account of British Jewry's Work for Victims of Nazi Oppression.* London: Cresset Press, 1956.

Berg, Mary. *The Diary of Mary Berg: Growing Up in the Warsaw Ghetto.* Edited by S. L. Shneiderman. Oxford, UK: Oneworld, 2009.

Bernadotte, Count Folke. *Last Days of the Reich: The Diary of Count Folke Bernadotte, October 1944–May 1945.* Introduction by Sune Persson. London: Frontline, 2009. First published by Cassell (London, 1945).

Białoszewski, Miron. *A Memoir of the Warsaw Uprising.* Translated by Madeline G. Levine. New York: New York Review Books, 2014.

Block, Gay, and Malka Drucker. *Rescuers: Portraits of Moral Courage in the Holocaust.* Prologue by Cynthia

Ozick. Afterword by Rabbi Harold M. Schulweis. New York: Holmes & Meier, 1992.

Boehm, Eric H. *We Survived: Fourteen Histories of the Hidden and Hunted in Nazi Germany.* Boulder, CO: Westview, 2003.

Brent, Leslie Baruch. *Sunday's Child? A Memoir.* New Romney, UK: Bank House Books, 2009.

Buchwalter, Marianne. *Memories of a Berlin Childhood.* Corvallis, OR: Premiere Editions International, 1995.

*Burger, Paula. As told to Andrea Jacobs. *Paula's Window: Papa, the Bielski Partisans, and a Life Unexpected. A Holocaust Memoir.* Denver: Paula Burger, 2014.

The Child Survivors' Association of Great Britain–AJR. *We Remember: Child Survivors of the Holocaust Speak.* Leicester, UK: Matador, 2011.

*David, Ruth. *Child of Our Time: A Young Girl's Flight from the Holocaust.* London: I. B. Tauris, 2002.

———. *Life-Lines.* London: self-published, 2011.

Dwork, Debórah, and Robert Jan Van Pelt. *Flight from the Reich: Refugee Jews, 1933–1946*. New York: W. W. Norton, 2009.

Engelmann, Bernt. *In Hitler's Germany: Everyday Life in the Third Reich*. Translated by Krishna Winston. New York: Schocken, 1986.

Evans, Richard J. *The Coming of the Third Reich*. New York: The Penguin Press, 2004.

Fairweather, Jack. *The Volunteer: One Man, An Underground Army, and the Secret Mission to Destroy Auschwitz*. New York: HarperCollins, 2019.

Fittko, Lisa. *Escape through the Pyrenees*. Translated by David Koblick. Evanston, IL: Northwestern University Press, 1991.

———. *Solidarity and Treason: Resistance and Exile, 1933–1940*. Evanston, IL: Northwestern University Press, 1995.

Gerhardt, Uta, and Thomas Karlauf, eds. *The Night of Broken Glass: Eyewitness Accounts of Kristallnacht*. Cambridge, UK: Polity Press, 2012.

Gilbert, Martin. *Kristallnacht: Prelude to Destruction.* New York: HarperCollins, 2006.

———. *The Righteous: The Unsung Heroes of the Holocaust.* New York: Henry Holt, 2003.

Goldberg, Rita. *Motherland: Growing Up with the Holocaust.* New York: The New Press, 2015.

Goldstein, Bernard. *Five Years in the Warsaw Ghetto (The Stars Bear Witness).* Translated and edited by Leonard Shatzkin. Oakland: Nabat/AK Press, 2005.

Gottlieb, Amy Zahl. *Men of Vision: Anglo-Jewry's Aid to Victims of the Nazi Regime, 1933–1945.* London: Weidenfeld & Nicolson, 1998.

Greenstein, Miriam K. *In the Shadow of Death: A Young Girl's Survival in the Holocaust.* Portland, OR: Press-22, 2010.

Grynberg, Michał, ed. *Words to Outlive Us: Eyewitness Accounts from the Warsaw Ghetto.* Translated by Philip Boehm. New York: Picador, 2003.

Gur, David. *Brothers for Resistance and Rescue: The Underground Zionist Youth Movement in Hungary during*

World War II. Edited by Eli Netzer. Translated by Pamela Segev and Avri Fischer. New York: Gefen, 2007.

Häsler, Alfred A. *The Lifeboat Is Full: Switzerland and the Refugees, 1933–1945.* New York: Funk & Wagnalls, 1967.

Kaplan, Marion A. *Between Dignity and Despair: Jewish Life in Nazi Germany.* New York: Oxford University Press, 1998.

Karski, Jan. *Story of a Secret State: My Report to the World.* Washington, DC: Georgetown University Press, 2013.

Kershaw, Ian. *Hitler: A Biography.* New York: W. W. Norton, 2010.

Klempner, Mark. *The Heart Has Reasons: Holocaust Rescuers and Their Stories of Courage.* Cleveland: Pilgrim Press, 2006.

Korczak, Janusz. *Ghetto Diary.* New Haven: Yale University Press, 2003.

Kubar, Zofia S. *Double Identity: A Memoir.* New York: Hill and Wang, 1989.

Laqueur, Walter. *Generation Exodus: The Fate of Young Jewish Refugees from Nazi Germany.* New York: I. B. Tauris, 2004.

Lazare, Lucien. *Rescue as Resistance: How Jewish Organizations Fought the Holocaust in France.* Translated by Jeffrey M. Green. New York: Columbia University Press, 1996.

Lewin, Abraham. *A Cup of Tears: A Diary of the Warsaw Ghetto.* Edited by Antony Polonsky. New York: Basil Blackwell, 1988.

Lixl-Purcell, Andreas, ed. *Women of Exile: German-Jewish Autobiographies since 1933.* New York: Greenwood, 1988.

Mark, Ber. *Uprising in the Warsaw Ghetto.* Translated by Gershon Friedlin. New York: Schocken, 1975.

*Meed, Vladka. *On Both Sides of the Wall.* Introduction by Elie Wiesel. Translated by Dr. Steven Meed. Washington, DC: Holocaust Library, 1999.

Michman, Jozeph, and Bert Jan Flim, eds. *The Encyclopedia of the Righteous Among the Nations: Rescuers of Jews during the Holocaust. The Netherlands.* Israel Gutman, Editor-in-chief. Jerusalem: Yad Vashem, 2004.

Museum of Jewish Heritage. *Daring to Resist: Jewish Defiance in the Holocaust*. New York: Museum of Jewish Heritage, 2007.

Nussbaum, Laureen, and Karen Kirtley. *Shedding Our Stars: The Story of Hans Calmeyer and How He Saved Thousands of Families Like Mine*. Berkeley, CA: She Writes Press, 2019.

Okrent, Daniel. *The Guarded Gate: Bigotry, Eugenics, and the Law That Kept Two Generations of Jews, Italians, and Other European Immigrants Out of America*. New York: Scribner, 2019.

Paldiel, Mordecai. *Saving the Jews: Amazing Stories of Men and Women Who Defied the "Final Solution."* Rockville, MD: Schreiber, 2000.

———. *Sheltering the Jews: Stories of Holocaust Rescuers*. Foreword by Franklin H. Littell. Minneapolis: Fortress Press, 1996.

Papanek, Ernst, with Edward Linn. *Out of the Fire*. New York: William Morrow, 1975.

Presser, Jacob. *Ashes in the Wind: The Destruction of Dutch*

Jewry. Translated by Arnold Pomerans. London: Souvenir, 2010.

*Rappaport, Doreen. *Beyond Courage: The Untold Story of Jewish Resistance during the Holocaust*. Somerville, MA: Candlewick, 2012.

*Rotem, Simha (Kazik). *Memoirs of a Warsaw Ghetto Fighter*. Translated and edited by Barbara Harshav. New Haven: Yale University Press, 1994.

Samuel, Vivette. *Rescuing the Children: A Holocaust Memoir*. Translated and with an introduction by Charles B. Paul. Foreword by Elie Wiesel. Madison: University of Wisconsin Press, 2002.

Semelin, Jacques. *The Survival of the Jews in France 1940–44*. Translated by Cynthia Schoch and Natasha Lehrer. New York: Oxford University Press, 2018.

Semelin, Jacques, Claire Andrieu, and Sarah Gensburger, eds. *Resisting Genocide: The Multiple Forms of Rescue*. Translated by Emma Bentley and Cynthia Schoch. New York: Oxford University Press, 2013.

Shirer, William L. *The Rise and Fall of the Third Reich*. New York: Fawcett Crest, 1983.

Steinberg, Lucien. *Jews against Hitler* (*Not As a Lamb*). Translated by Marion Hunter. London: Gordon & Cremonesi, 1978.

Stevens, Michael E., ed. *Remembering the Holocaust*. Madison: Wisconsin Historical Society, 1997.

Suhl, Yuri, ed. and trans. *They Fought Back: The Story of the Jewish Resistance in Nazi Europe*. New York: Schocken, 1978.

Szwajger, Adina Blady. *I Remember Nothing More: The Warsaw Children's Hospital and the Jewish Resistance*. Translated from the Polish by Tasja Darowska and Danusia Stok. New York: Touchstone, 1992.

*Vrba, Rudolf, and Alan Bestic. *I Cannot Forgive*. New York: Bantam, 1964.

Wachsmann, Nikolaus. *KL: A History of the Nazi Concentration Camps*. New York: Farrar, Straus and Giroux, 2015.

Weitz, Margaret Collins. *Sisters in the Resistance: How Women Fought to Free France, 1940–1945*. New York: John Wiley & Sons, 1995.

Zandman, Felix, with David Chanoff. *Never the Last Journey*. New York: Schocken, 1995.

Ziemian, Joseph. *The Cigarette Sellers of Three Crosses Square*. Translated by Janina David. Minneapolis: Lerner, 1975.

ORAL HISTORY INTERVIEWS, UNPUBLISHED ACCOUNTS, AND MEMOIRS

Alpert, Pela Rosen. Oral History. Courtesy of the Wisconsin Historical Society, Wisconsin Survivors of the Holocaust. Interviews and photographs, circa 1939–circa 1945, 1974–1975, 1980–1981. Interview dates January 30, 1974; June 5, 1975; March 5, 1980.

Angress, Fred. "Survival in the Lion's Den." Courtesy of the Leo Baeck Institute, New York, May 11, 1989.

Brawerman, George. "On the Fringes of the Holocaust." Courtesy of the Leo Baeck Institute, New York.

DeLevie, Herb. Oral History. Courtesy of the Wisconsin Historical Society, Wisconsin Survivors of the Holocaust. Interviews and photographs, circa 1939–circa 1945, 1974–1975, 1980–1981. Interview dates March 11, 1980; March 13, 1980; March 20, 1980.

Deutschkron, Eva. Oral History. Courtesy of the Wisconsin Historical Society, Wisconsin Survivors of the Holocaust. Interviews and photographs, circa 1939–circa 1945, 1974–1975, 1980–1981. Interview dates September 3 and 5, 1980.

Edmands, Eva Rappart. "Childhood Memoirs of World War II." Courtesy of the Leo Baeck Institute, New York, June 26, 1997.

Hiller, Gunter. Transcript, Gunter Hiller (1928–) Oral History Interview #717, 8/05/1993, by David Turner, Oregon Jewish Museum and Center for Holocaust Education.

Kaufmann, Burt. "Letter." Courtesy of the Leo Baeck Institute, New York, 1945.

Kurz, Bronka Harz. "Bronka Harz Kurz memoir." Accession Number: 2006.6. United States Holocaust Memorial Museum, December 8, 2005.

Liebmann, Max K. "Odyssee to Switzerland." Courtesy of the Leo Baeck Institute, New York, 2001.

Meed, Benjamin. USHMM, Ghettos, Personal Histories, United States Holocaust Memorial Museum, https://

www.ushmm.org/exhibition/personal-history/media_oi.php?MediaId=1096.

Moritz, Alfred. "Survival." Courtesy of the Leo Baeck Institute, New York, 2000.

Münzer, Alfred. Oral history interview with Alfred Münzer, courtesy of the United States Holocaust Memorial Museum. Oral History. Accession Number: 2002.181. RG Number: RG-50.106.0156. August 4, 2002.

Newman, Gerald F. "Miraculous Survival." Courtesy of the Leo Baeck Institute, New York, circa 1980.

Robert, Arthur. Transcript, Arthur Robert Oral History Interview #803, August 2, 1993, by Jeffrey Lang, Oregon Jewish Museum and Center for Holocaust Education.

Rodbell, Barbara Ledermann. Oral History Interview. Accession Number 1990.409.1. RG Number: RG-50.030.0192. United States Holocaust Memorial Museum, June 12, 1990.

Sonnenberg, Gertrud. "Story of a Survivor." Courtesy of the Leo Baeck Institute, New York, 1985.

Weinberg, Lisl. "Susie's Story." Courtesy of the Leo Baeck Institute, New York, 1978.

Zawacki, Leonard. Transcript, Leonard Zawacki (1916–2001) Oral History Interview #779, 07/17/1992, by Oregon Holocaust Resource Center, Oregon Jewish Museum and Center for Holocaust Education.

NEWSPAPERS, JOURNAL ARTICLES, AND WEBSITES

Bell, Leslie. "Mystery Bielski Remembered," *New American,* August 1, 2014, https://www.thenewamerican.com /culture/history/item/18792-mystery-bielski -remembered.

Berger, Joseph. "Vladka Meed, Who Infiltrated Warsaw Ghetto, Dies at 90," *New York Times,* November 24, 2012, https://www.nytimes.com/2012/11/25/world /vladka-meed-who-infiltrated-warsaw-ghetto -dies-at-90.html.

"The Bielski Partisans," USHMM Holocaust Encyclopedia, https://encyclopedia.ushmm.org/content/en /article/the-bielski-partisans.

Borzykowski, T. "The Last Passover in the Warsaw Ghetto," Yad Vashem, https://www.yadvashem.org/yv/en/exhibitions/warsaw_ghetto_testimonies/last_passover.asp.

Crouch, Gregory. "Frederik Philips Dies at 100; Businessman Saved Dutch Jews," *New York Times*, December 7, 2005, https://www.nytimes.com/2005/12/07/business/frederik-philips-dies-at-100-businessman-saved-dutch-jews.html.

Deutschkron obituary: https://www.cressfuneralservice.com/obituary/30560/Eva-Deutschkron-of-Madison-WI/.

Fox, Margalit. "Benjamin Meed, 88, Who Was a Key Advocate for Holocaust Survivors, Dies," *New York Times*, October 26, 2006, https://www.nytimes.com/2006/10/26/obituaries/26meed.html.

Gerrie, Anthea. "We Fell in Love in a Concentration Camp," *New York Post*, April 7, 2018, https://nypost.com/2018/04/07/how-this-couples-love-endured-the-holocaust/.

Jerusalem Post. "David Gur." April 15, 2007, https://www.jpost.com/Israel/David-Gur.

Martin, Douglas. "Lisa Fittko, Who Helped Rescue Many Who Fled the Nazis, Dies at 95," *New York Times*, March 21, 2005, https://www.nytimes.com/2005/03/21/obituaries/lisa-fittko-who-helped-rescue-many-who-fled-the-nazis-dies-at-95.html.

New York Times. "Zielenziger, Eric W. Obituary," November 21, 2010, https://www.legacy.com/obituaries/nytimes/obituary.aspx?n=eric-w-zielenziger&pid=146717925.

POLIN Museum of the History of Polish Jews, https://sztetl.org.pl/en/towns/k/812-kolomyia/99-history/137492-history-of-community.

Poznanski, Renée. "Was the French Resistance Jewish?" *Tablet*, May 6, 2016, https://www.tabletmag.com/jewish-arts-and-culture/books/201308/was-the-french-resistance-jewish.

Reiniger, Franziska, "Solidarity in the Forest—The Bielski Brothers," Yad Vashem, https://www.yadvashem.org/articles/general/solidarity-bielski-brothers.html.

Ringelblum, Emanuel. "The Oneg Shabbat Archives," https://www.yadvashem.org/yv/en/exhibitions/ringelblum/index.asp.

Saidel, Rochelle G. "Vladka Meed 1921–2012," Jewish Women's Archive, The Encyclopedia of Jewish Women, https://jwa.org/encyclopedia/article/meed -vladka.

Seelye, Katharine, Q. "A Doomed Ghetto Lives in a Time Capsule of Art and Desperation," *New York Times*, September 8, 1998, https://www.nytimes.com /1998/09/08/arts/a-doomed-ghetto-lives-in-a-time -capsule-of-art-and-desperation.html.

Sheffield, Dr. Gary. "The Fall of France." BBC. Last updated 2011-03-30, https://www.bbc.co.uk/history /worldwars/wwtwo/fall_france_01.shtml.

Vitello, Paul. "Leo Bretholz, 93, Dies; Escaped Train to Auschwitz," *New York Times*, March 29, 2014, https:// www.nytimes.com/2014/03/30/world/europe /leo-bretholz-93-dies-escaped-train-to-auschwitz .html.

The Wiener Library for the Study of the Holocaust and Genocide. "Auschwitz-Birkenau," The Holocaust Explained, https://www.theholocaustexplained.org /the-final-solution/auschwitz-birkenau/kanada -kommando.

SOURCE NOTES
(CLUES TO HIDDEN TREASURES)

If you're here, congratulations! You have the making of a history detective. Source notes might seem boring, but they do matter. Source notes are like the clues in an old treasure map, leading us to riches and to stories that help expand the way we see the world. When I see an intriguing quotation in a book, I always check the source note. Many times, I discover a fascinating new primary source to help me with my research.

For this book, I'm grateful to have access to primary oral histories and transcripts of interviews with Holocaust survivors. That is only possible thanks to the many volunteers and staff of museums, libraries, and historical societies who work to preserve these testimonies and make them accessible by transcribing tapes or videos and digitalizing first-person accounts.

Excerpts from oral histories and unpublished manuscripts are courtesy of the following organizations: the Leo Baeck Institute, New York; the United States Holocaust Memorial Museum (USHMM); the Oregon Jewish Museum and Center for Holocaust Education (OJMCHE); and the Wisconsin Historical Society. The first citation follows the format requested by the source; in subsequent citations, sources are abbreviated.

"When a country is overcome . . .": Semelin, et al., *Resisting Genocide*, 1.

INTRODUCTION

"And now I see . . .": Fittko, *Solidarity and Treason*, 5.

BERLIN, 1933

Lisa Fittko: Martin, "Lisa Fittko, Who Helped Rescue Many Who Fled the Nazis, Dies at 95," *New York Times*, March 21, 2005, https://www .nytimes.com/2005/03/21/obituaries/lisa-fittko-who-helped-rescue -many-who-fled-the-nazis-dies-at-95.html.

TO GIVE THE DEAD A VOICE . . .

"'When you have worked . . .'": Presser, *Ashes in the Wind*. This translation of an interview with Dr. Presser by Philo Bregstein appears in the Afterword by Dienke Hondius, 555–556.

DEAR READER

"'I want you to be upset . . .'": Kryszek, transcript, Chella Velt Meekcoms Kryszek (1928–2013) oral history interview by Shirley Tanzer. Transcribed by Unknown. January 27–28, 1976, OJCMHEC, 53. (Pagination is based on printed copy of online transcript.)
"Like history, life continues . . .": Presser, 545.

Part One

"It is important . . .": Angress, F. "Survival in the Lions' Den," Courtesy of the Leo Baeck Institute, New York, 1.
"I had an open look . . .": Bader, Oral History, Wisconsin Historical Society, Wisconsin Survivors of the Holocaust. Interviews and photographs, circa 1939–circa 1945, 1974–1975, 1980–1981. Interview conducted by Jean Loeb Lettofsky, November 17 and November 19, 1980, 55.

Hitler Youth: *Encyclopedia Britannica*, "Hitler Youth," https://www
.britannica.com/topic/Hitler-Youth.

CHAPTER ONE

"Once we were in hiding . . .": Deutschkron, Oral History, Wisconsin
Historical Society, Wisconsin Survivors of the Holocaust. Interviews
and photographs, circa 1939–circa 1945, 1974–1975, 1980–1981.
Interview conducted by Jean Loeb Lettofsky, September 3 and
September 5, 1980, 63.

"Because we absolutely refused . . .": ibid., 15.

Global rise of antisemitism: ADL, https://www.adl.org/news
/press-releases/adl-global-survey-of-18-countries-finds-hardcore-anti
-semitic-attitudes-remain.

"'I can't see you anymore . . .'": ibid., 16.

"Jews could not be 'Aryan,' . . .": David, *Child of Our Time*, 15.

"Hundreds died in the camps . . .": USHMM Holocaust Encyclopedia,
"Kristallnacht," USHMM, https://encyclopedia.ushmm.org/content
/en/article/kristallnacht.

"I had to go out, make all the arrangements . . .": Deutschkron, 20.

"We were fighting for our life . . .": ibid., 24.

"By this time . . .": ibid., 25.

Ruth Hirschhahn: Yad Vashem Central Database of Shoah Victims'
Names: https://yvng.yadvashem.org/index.html?language=en&s
_lastName=hirschhahn&s_firstName=Ruth&s_place=&s
_dateOfBirth= ; also https://www.geni.com/people/Ruth-Hirschhahn
/6000000000795127943.

"This was the end of their strength . . .": Deutschkron, 25.

"We knew there were labor camps . . .": ibid., 33.

"Instead, the Holocaust was . . .": Wachsmann, *KL*, 292.

"I was making ammunition . . .": Deutschkron, 26.

"Our apartment was on the fourth . . .": ibid., 34.

"So he went then to my parents . . .": ibid., 34–35.

"I saw him standing there . . .": ibid., 35.

"I couldn't go up to him . . .": ibid.

"'You are young . . .'": ibid.

"'They shall not get us . . .'": ibid., 52.

"He was not Jewish . . .": ibid., 38.

"'You are hiding . . .'": ibid.

"Martin became Franz . . .": ibid.

"'I work in this department . . .'": ibid., 39.

"So Martin really went . . .": ibid.

"And this fellow felt very sorry . . .": ibid., 39–40.

"So we went . . .": ibid., 44.

"I remember that I felt . . .": ibid., 50.

"Of course, nobody . . .": ibid., 63.

"But it didn't come . . .": ibid.

"I started crying . . .": ibid., 58.

"'Don't worry . . .'": ibid.

"We just lived . . .": ibid., 85.

Eva Deutschkron obituary: https://www.cressfuneralservice.com /obituary/30560/Eva-Deutschkron-of-Madison-WI.

CHAPTER TWO

"Our hunger was so great . . .": Sonnenberg, "Story of a Survivor," courtesy of Leo Baeck Institute, New York, 1985, 6.

"My sister Herta . . .": ibid., 4.

"My sister and I . . .": ibid.

"Germans first and Jewish last . . .": ibid., 5.

"We were told to be prepared . . .": ibid.

"Then they sent us . . .": ibid.

"The Germans saw the ghettos . . .": USHMM Holocaust Encyclopedia,

"Ghettos," USHMM, https://encyclopedia.ushmm.org/content/en/article/ghettos.

"We were told . . .": Sonnenberg, 6.

"The Germans did not hesitate . . .": USHMM Holocaust Encyclopedia, "Ghettos," USHMM, https://encyclopedia.ushmm.org/content/en/article/ghettos.

Final Solution: USHMM Holocaust Encyclopedia, "Final Solution," USHMM, https://encyclopedia.ushmm.org/content/en/article/the-final-solution.

"I was sent to shovel . . .": Sonnenberg, 6.

"Whenever there was to be . . .": ibid.

"In all of the misery . . .": ibid., 11.

"You played games . . .": DeLevie, Oral History, Wisconsin Historical Society, Wisconsin Survivors of the Holocaust. Interviews and photographs, circa 1939–circa 1945, 1974–1975, 1980–1981. Interview conducted by Sara Leuchter, March 11, 1980; March 13, 1980; March 20, 1980, 35–36. https://www.wisconsinhistory.org/HolocaustSurvivors/DeLevie.asp.

"My mother told my sister . . .": Sonnenberg,7.

"When I received the note . . .": ibid.

"'Dear children . . .'": ibid.

"We tried to sell . . .": ibid., 6.

"The sun glinted . . .": ibid., 8.

"There were SS . . .": ibid.

"The SS were coming . . .": ibid.

"During the walk . . .": ibid.

"He had been told . . .": ibid.

"Had Count Bernadotte . . .": ibid., 10.

"They practically had to push . . .": ibid.

"'When the doors open . . .'": ibid.

"We didn't believe it . . .": ibid.

"We were people . . .": ibid.

"We were nursed . . .": ibid.

"In the beginning . . .": ibid., 11.

CHAPTER THREE

"If you want to stay alive . . .": Angress, F., 31.

"My brothers and I . . .": ibid., 1.

"Some of my former classmates . . .": ibid.

seas of flags: Angress, W., *Witness to the Storm*, 80.

"Later in the United States . . .": ibid., 79–80.

"Papa was reluctant . . .": ibid., 80.

"I remember the years . . .": Angress, F., 5.

"My parents tried hard . . .": Angress, W., 200.

"I remember it vividly . . ." Angress, F., 5.

"We were shocked . . .": ibid.

"We made several attempts . . .": ibid., 6.

Jewish population in the Netherlands: USHMM Holocaust
    Encyclopedia, "The Netherlands," USHMM, https://encyclopedia
    .ushmm.org/content/en/article/the-netherlands.

"'Frau Angress, if YOU . . .'": Angress, F., 7.

"We Dutch Jews . . .": Bader, 50.

"But what could she do . . .": Angress, F., 11.

"She was terribly worried . . .": ibid.

"The members of the . . .": USHMM Holocaust Encyclopedia, "Jewish
    Councils," USHMM, https://encyclopedia.ushmm.org/content/en
    /article/jewish-councils-judenraete.

"We tried to sabotage . . .": Angress, F., 15.

"I happened to come across . . .": ibid., 16.

"The horrors we had hoped . . .": ibid., 8.

"But all our efforts . . .": ibid., 22.

"He would first treat . . .": ibid.

"One particular night stands out . . .": ibid., 23.

"Just as I very quietly . . .": ibid.

"Walter Süskind had alerted . . .": ibid., 24.

"From there they were be placed . . .": ibid.

June 20, 1943 raid: Presser, 206–207.

"I had to find . . .": Angress, F., 27.

"The scene was indescribable . . .": ibid., 29.

"I would never forget . . .": ibid., 30.

"If he were in our shoes . . .": ibid., 31.

"the total liquidation . . ."; Jewish Council disbanded: Presser, 213–214.

"'Abraham, this is it! . . .'": Angress, F., 31.

"Going into hiding . . .": ibid., 32.

"With a big smile . . .": ibid.

"'Going under' involved . . .": ibid., 34.

"They also got . . .": ibid.

"We ate onions . . .": ibid., 35.

"On March 24, 1944 . . .": ibid., 37.

"From the moment I entered . . .": ibid.

"The days in hiding . . .": ibid., 38.

"The Jews went quickly . . .": Kaufmann, B., "Letter," courtesy of the
    Leo Baeck Institute, New York, 7.

"Sometimes it was a problem . . .": ibid.

"A few days before Christmas . . .": Kaufmann, 8.

"Most people had nothing . . .": ibid.

"And there were those times . . .": Angress, F., 42.

"Instead of keeping a low profile . . .": ibid., 45.

"Forty-three years . . .": ibid., 51.

"One of the speakers . . .": ibid., 52.

"To Nelly Gispen . . .": ibid., dedication.

CHAPTER FOUR

"We are going to carry . . .": Kryszek, 34.

"I lost so much that was dear . . .": ibid., 53.

"young people have a duty . . .": ibid., 75.

"Because Holland is a very small distance . . .": ibid., 4.

"People, if they spoke up . . .": ibid., 6.

Dutch strike: USHMM Holocaust Encyclopedia, "The Netherlands," USHMM, https://encyclopedia.ushmm.org/content/en/article /the-netherlands.

"I went berserk . . .": Kryszek, 7.

"'I'm from the Dutch underground . . .'": ibid.

"We didn't sleep that night . . .": ibid.

"Your heart stopped in your throat . . .": ibid., 10.

"'What will happen now . . .'": ibid.

"If someone had coughed . . .": ibid., 12.

"'Open the door!'": ibid., 14.

"'Oh, my little girl . . .'": ibid.

"'It was very foolish . . .'": ibid., 15.

"'We've come to get . . .'": ibid., 16.

"'It's my dream . . .'": ibid.

"'It is true . . .'": ibid.

Number of Jews deported: USHMM Holocaust Encyclopedia, "The Netherlands," USHMM, https://encyclopedia.ushmm.org/content/en /article/the-netherlands.

"I felt all the time . . .": Kryszek, 18.

"'My life hangs on that cable . . .'": ibid.

"In the other cell . . .": ibid., 19-20.

"'Look, there is only one thing . . .'": ibid., 19.

"That saved me.": ibid., 20.

"People asked me afterwards . . .": ibid., 23.

"'You come and find me . . .'": ibid., 22.

"'Anything you want to do . . .'": ibid., 24.

Israel Velt: https://www.findagrave.com/memorial/131670439
/israel-salomon-velt.

Philips: Crouch, "Frederick Philips Dies at 100; Businessman Saved
Dutch Jews," *New York Times*, December 7, 2005.

"Mr. Philips had flown . . .": Kryszek, 26.

"The truth about Nazi . . .": Wachsmann, 306.

"We were in those cattle wagons . . .": Kryszek, 26.

"Many, of course . . .": ibid.

"One day I wouldn't eat . . .": ibid., 28.

"I thought, 'If we go . . .'": ibid.

"Many, many years . . .": ibid., 29.

Canada Commando: Auschwitz-Birkenau, Wiener Library for the Study
of the Holocaust and Genocide, https://www.theholocaustexplained
.org/the-final-solution/auschwitz-birkenau/kanada-kommando.

"Some new arrivals . . .": Wachsmann, 310–311.

"'choiceless choices.'": ibid., 311.

"I really prayed . . .": Kryszek, 29.

"There was no pity.": ibid.

"We were going insane . . .": ibid.

"We were there . . .": ibid., 30.

"'God, if you are listening . . .'": ibid., 31.

"It was the same type . . .": ibid., 31.

"I remember the little children . . .": ibid.

"She made such a big impression . . .": ibid.

"We didn't really want . . .": ibid.

"'Oh, you are so fortunate . . .'": ibid., 33.

"we really wanted . . .": ibid.

"I made her get out . . .": ibid., 34.

"'Shoot me. Shoot me, please . . .'": ibid.

"'You are going to walk . . .'": ibid.

"'Let's sing songs . . .'": ibid., 35.

"'These are for my sister . . .'": ibid.

"We all knew each other . . .": ibid., 38.

"One day in the beginning . . .": ibid., 40.

"They said to us in German . . .": ibid.

"We were like walking skeletons . . .": ibid., 41.

"Well, that's when I started . . .": ibid., 42.

"I remember walking by the door . . .": ibid., 44.

"I'm very grateful . . .": ibid., 44–45.

"He used to say to me . . .": ibid., 66.

Part Two

"My childhood was not unusual . . .": David, *Child of Our Time*,
   dedication page.

CHAPTER FIVE

"Absolutely no one . . .": Moritz, A., "Survival: 1933–1945," courtesy of
   the Leo Baeck Institute, New York, 27.

"The thugs threw everything . . .": ibid., 43.

"He announced that anyone . . .": ibid.

"tough old bird . . .": ibid, 45.

"I was overwhelmed . . .": ibid., 27.

Removal of Alfred Moritz's name: ibid., 13.

Number of Jews in France: USHMM Holocaust Encyclopedia, "France,"
   USHMM, https://encyclopedia.ushmm.org/content/en/article/france.

"Their kindness gave us . . .": Moritz, 65.

Drancy: USHMM Holocaust Encyclopedia, "Drancy," USHMM, https:
//encyclopedia.ushmm.org/content/en/article/drancy.

"We found ourselves . . .": Moritz, 73, 75.

"'Go away with those . . .'": ibid., 75.

"On July 4, 1942 . . .": ibid., 79.

"After a few weeks . . .": ibid., 85.

"He scraped the butter . . .": ibid., 89.

"It was decided . . .": ibid.

"Our woman escort hissed . . .": ibid., 99.

"The fear had been . . .": ibid.

"He belonged to the 'Garel group' . . .": ibid., 101.

Georges Garel: Poznanski, R., "Was the French Resistance Jewish?,"
Tablet, May 3, 2016, https://www.tabletmag.com/jewish-arts
-and-culture/books/201308/was-the-french-resistance-jewish.

"took both daring and guts." Moritz, 101.

"They ate delicious-looking . . .": ibid.

"We tried to look our hungriest . . .": ibid.

"Wandering about the station entrance . . .": ibid., 105.

"a wild land of goats . . .": ibid., 109.

"thugs with obviously sick . . .": ibid.

"The house was divided . . .": ibid., 113.

"Barefoot in our straw-filled . . .": ibid., 125.

"Our teacher, Mr. Gounod . . .": ibid.

"Here we were, naked . . .": ibid., 128.

"He said he knew . . .": ibid., 145.

"We didn't cry . . .": ibid.

"The rapid advance . . .": ibid.

"'We were very surprised . . .'": ibid., 157.

"self-sufficient, hardened and emotionally tough . . .": ibid., 163.

"WE THEN REALIZED . . .": ibid., 165.

"After the war . . .": ibid., 177.

Ernest Moritz obituary: *South Florida Sun Sentinel*, September 7, 2010, https://www.sun-sentinel.com/news/fl-xpm-2010-09-07-fl-ernest -moritz-obit-20100907-story.html#; Alfred Moritz obituary information: https://www.findagrave.com/memorial/142424027 /alfred-moritz.

"I felt a shock . . .": Moritz, 1.

CHAPTER SIX

"All of a sudden . . .": Liebmann, M., "Odyssee [Odyssey] to Switzerland," courtesy of the Leo Baeck Institute, New York, 14.

"We climbed all day . . .": ibid., 13.

"'HALT!'": ibid., 14.

"It did not take too long . . .": ibid., 4.

"The result of this fight . . .": ibid.

"We were constantly under . . .": ibid., 4–5.

"The next morning . . .": ibid., 8.

"With very few exceptions . . .": ibid.

"There were 25 barracks . . .": ibid., 9.

"People were demoralized . . . Medical problems . . .": ibid.

"'There was no privacy . . .'": Gerrie, A., "We Fell in Love in a Concentration Camp," *New York Post*, April 7, 2018, https://nypost.com /2018/04/07/how-this-couples-love-endured-the-holocaust.

"She loved me enough . . .": Hirsch Liebmann, Oral History Interview, United States Holocaust Memorial Museum, 1990, https://encyclopedia.ushmm.org/content/en/oral-history/hanne -hirsch-liebmann-describes-a-childrens-aid-society-ose-visit -and-life-in-le-chambon-sur-lignon.

"On August 6, the first . . .": Liebmann, 12.

"'Two days later . . .'": Gerrie, "We Fell in Love . . . ," *New York Post*.

"'Where can I find . . .'": Liebmann, 12.

"Hanne was one of them . . .": ibid., 12–13.

"Mme. Philip told me . . .": ibid., 13.

"We went by train . . .": ibid.

"'HALT!'" ibid., 14.

"We arrived in New York . . .": ibid., 17.

"'We were so overwhelmed . . .'": Gerrie, "We Fell in Love . . . ," *New York Post*.

CHAPTER SEVEN

"I do not believe . . .": David, *Life-Lines*, 11.

"The picture of the Führer . . .": David, *Child of Our Time*, 14.

"In Mannheim the synagogue . . .": ibid, 49, 52.

"Surprisingly, in the spring . . .": ibid., 118.

"In their letters . . . :" ibid.,123.

"In March 1941 my parents were taken . . ." David, *Life-Lines*, 105.

"Conditions were also cruel . . .": David, *Child of Our Time*, 125.

"My younger sister . . .": ibid.

"'It is nearly three years . . . '": ibid., 125–126.

"Still known as VE Day . . .": ibid., 144.

"Mother pushed an old . . .": David, *Life-Lines*, 170.

Part Three

"Around me there was so much pain . . .": Szwajger, *I Remember Nothing More*, 136.

CHAPTER EIGHT

"'We are lost, Papa . . .'": Burger, P., *Paula's Window*, 62.

"A child can get lost . . .": ibid., 9.

"Then, on a summer day . . .": ibid., 17.

"Jews lost all citizenship rights . . .": ibid., 17–18.

"He knew when . . .": ibid., 20.

"German authorities killed . . .": USHMM Holocaust Encyclopedia, "The Bielski Partisans," USHMM, https://encyclopedia.ushmm.org /content/en/article/the-bielski-partisans.

"We could take only a few . . .": Burger, 21.

"Isaac bobbed up and down . . .": ibid., 22.

"I can still see . . .": ibid., 23–24.

"'If anything happens to me . . .'": ibid., 24.

"I stopped asking . . .": ibid., 31.

"'I am taking you . . .'": ibid., 32.

"To avoid discovery . . .": ibid.

"My father, ashen and overwhelmed . . .": ibid., 33.

Yehuda Bielski: USHMM, photograph of Yehuda Bielski in the forest, https://collections.ushmm.org/search/catalog/pa1176984.

fifth brother: Bell, L., "Mystery Bielski Remembered," *New American*, August 1, 2014, 6, https://www.thenewamerican.com/culture/history /item/18792-mystery-bielski-remembered.

"a statuesque, handsome man . . .": ibid., 38–39.

"Far less dangerous . . .": ibid., 41.

"Tuvia ordered . . .": ibid., 41–42.

"The artist in me . . .": ibid., 39.

"One morning I opened the tent . . .": ibid., 40.

"After felling trees . . .": ibid., 52.

"The base camp . . .": Bell, 6.

"In a desperate rescue attempt . . .": Reiniger, F. "Solidarity in the Forest—The Bielski Brothers," Yad Vashem, https://www.yadvashem .org/articles/general/solidarity-bielski-brothers.html.

"Tuvia repeatedly warned . . .": Burger, 60.

"We waded deeper and deeper . . .": ibid., 61.

"'Keep going . . .'": ibid.

"'We are lost . . .'": ibid., 62.

"We had a school . . .": ibid., 68.

"'Before we start . . .'": ibid., 74.

"Tuvia Bielski . . .": ibid., 76.

"'Thank you for saving . . .'": ibid., 113.

"'Don't rush to fight . . .'": Reiniger, quoting from Nechama, Tec,
    Defiance: The True Story of the Bielski Partisans (Oxford: Oxford University
    Press, 1993), 112.

"'I'll be famous . . .'": ibid.

CHAPTER NINE

"We escaped to the woods . . .": Kurz, B., "Letter," United States
    Holocaust Memorial Museum, December 8, 2005, 2.

"To Whom It May Concern . . .": ibid.,1.

"Shortly after their arrival . . .": ibid.

"Thereafter we were ordered . . .": ibid.

"Intermittently the Germans made raids . . .": ibid.

"all the people . . .": ibid., 2.

"Finally, it became apparent . . .": ibid.

"In March 1942, Germans created . . .": "Kolomyia," POLIN Museum of
    the History of Polish Jews, https://sztetl.org.pl/en/towns/k/812
    -kolomyia/99-history/137492-history-of-community.

"They decided to get . . .": Kurz, 2..

"I begged my mother . . .": ibid.

"Miraculously we were returned . . .": ibid.

"We were frequently homeless . . .": ibid.

"Finally in 1944 . . .": ibid., 3.

Columbia University School of Social Alumni Newsletter, http://www
.columbia.edu/cu/ssw/alumni/notes/notesFY18NewsJuly.html.

CHAPTER TEN

"These bits of paper . . .": Robertson, W., "Surviving in Warsaw—My
Wartime Experiences," in *We Remember*, 148.

Lucjan Blit: YIVO Institute for Jewish Research, http://www
.yivoarchives.org/index.php?p=collections/controlcard&id=33315.

Warsaw ghetto established: USHMM Holocaust Encyclopedia,
"Warsaw Ghetto," USHMM, https://encyclopedia.ushmm.org/content
/en/article/warsaw.

"A high brick wall . . ." Robertson, 148.

Seven people to a room: USHMM, "Warsaw Ghetto," Holocaust
Encyclopedia, USHMM, https://encyclopedia.ushmm.org/content/en
/article/warsaw.

"Conditions in the Ghetto . . .": Robertson, 148.

"Then posters appeared . . .": ibid.

"But as we watched . . .": ibid.

"My family built . . .": ibid.

"The decision that we . . .": ibid., 149.

"At night we were smuggled . . .": ibid.

"Mrs. Dubiel, a kindly old Pole . . .": Meed, V., *On Both Sides of the Wall*, 112.

"Both girls were greatly distressed . . .": ibid.

"Thereafter she had haunted . . .": ibid., 112–113.

"The girls accepted my warning . . .": ibid., 113.

CHAPTER ELEVEN

"'Weapons, give us weapons!'": ibid., 122.

"The goal for which . . .": ibid., 94.

"Warsaw, July 22, 1942 . . .": ibid., 9.

"The letters leaped . . .": ibid., 13.

"'By order of the German . . .'": ibid.

Treblinka: USHMM Holocaust Encyclopedia, "Killing Centers: An Overview," USHMM, https://encyclopedia.ushmm.org/content/en /article/killing-centers-an-overview.

"Between July 22 . . .": USHMM Holocaust Encyclopedia, "Warsaw Ghetto Uprising," USHMM, https://encyclopedia.ushmm.org/content /en/article/warsaw-ghetto-uprising.

"Throughout each day . . .": Meed, V., 43.

"I was alone now . . .": ibid., 47.

armed resistance groups: USHMM Holocaust Encyclopedia, "Warsaw Ghetto Uprising," USHMM, https://encyclopedia.ushmm.org/content /en/article/warsaw-ghetto-uprising.

"But escape was easier . . .": Meed, V., 76.

"My blood ran cold . . .": ibid., 77.

"At that moment . . .": ibid., 78.

"As a result . . .": ibid., 83.

"'Very well, let's go . . .'": ibid., 92.

"I started a new life . . .": ibid., 85.

"Very little could be . . .": ibid., 122.

"It was difficult to get . . .": ibid., 126.

"under the noses . . .": ibid., 125.

"The early spring . . .": ibid., 133.

"I couldn't jump . . .": ibid., 134.

"Jews now would resist . . .": ibid., 137.

CHAPTER TWELVE

"The entire sky of Warsaw was red . . .": Meed, B., USHMM "Ghettos," Personal Histories, USHMM, https://www.ushmm.org/exhibition /personal-history/media_oi.php?MediaId=1096.

"'No one slept that night . . .'": Borzykowski, T. "The Last Passover in the Warsaw Ghetto," Yad Vashem, https://www.yadvashem.org/yv /en/exhibitions/warsaw_ghetto_testimonies/last_passover.asp. Quoted from Borzykowski, T., *Between Tumbling Walls*, 48.

"The ghetto was surrounded . . .": Meed, V., 140.

"Finally, the time had come . . .": Rotem, S., *Memoirs of a Warsaw Ghetto Fighter*, 33.

"I saw and I didn't believe . . .": ibid., 34.

"On the sixth day . . .": Meed, V., 143.

"The entire sky . . .": Meed. B., USHMM, "Personal Histories," USHMM, https://www.ushmm.org/exhibition/personal-history /media_oi.php?MediaId=1096.

"Reaching the house . . .": Meed, V., 143.

"Though German forces . . .": USHMM Holocaust Encyclopedia, "Warsaw Ghetto Uprising," USHMM, https://encyclopedia.ushmm .org/content/en/article/warsaw-ghetto-uprising.

Stroop casualty estimates: ibid.

"It was hard for me to believe . . .": Rotem, 45.

"Their hollow, haunted eyes . . .": Meed, V., 148.

"'Something has happened . . .'": ibid., 155.

"'Keep well. Perhaps we'll see . . .'": ibid.

"When the fighting . . .": ibid., 163.

"The Dubiels became afraid . . .": Robertson, in *We Remember*, 150.

"Very few Jewish . . .": Meed, V., 182.

"When the Russian soldiers . . .": Robertson, in *We Remember*, 151.

"We went to school . . .": Robertson, E-mail to author, January 31, 2019.

"I would tell . . .": ibid.

EPILOGUE

"It must all be recorded . . .": Ringelblum, Oneg Shabbat Archives, https://www.yadvashem.org/yv/en/exhibitions/ringelblum/index.asp.

"If that evil had conquered . . .": Bretholz, quoted in Vitello, "Leo Bretholz, 93, Dies; Escaped Train to Auschwitz," https://www.nytimes.com/2014/03/30/world/europe/leo-bretholz-93-dies-escaped-train-to-auschwitz.html, March 29, 2014.

"It was night . . .": Brawerman, G., "On the Fringe of the Holocaust," courtesy of the Leo Baeck Institute, New York, 21.

"I don't know . . .": Rodbell, B., Interview with Barbara Ledermann Rodbell, USHMM, 31.

"On May 8, 1945 . . .": Angress, F., 43–44.

"When Mutti [mother] and I . . .": Angress, W., *Witness to the Storm*, 320.

"Quiet, heart! Stop racing so . . .": Meed, V., 261–262.

"We must tell our story . . .": Meed, B., "Benjamin Meed,: USHMM Holocaust Encyclopedia, USHMM, https://encyclopedia.ushmm.org/content/en/article/benjamin-meed.

PHOTOGRAPH PERMISSIONS

Photos ©: age fotostock: cover (Buyenlarge/UIG); Courtesy of the Leo Baeck Institute: 28; Ruth David at the National Holocaust Centre and Museum, UK: 171; Courtesy Oregon Jewish Museum and Center for Holocaust Education: 76, 77; United States Holocaust Memorial Museum: 118, 120, 137 (courtesy of Alfred Moritz), v, 72 left, 72 right (courtesy of Alfred Munzer), 34 (courtesy of Amichai (Max) Heppner), 127, 266 (courtesy of Andre Limot), 45 (courtesy of Barbara Ledermann Rodbell), 250 (courtesy of Beit Lohamei Haghetaot (Ghetto Fighters' House Museum), 15 (courtesy of Bella Rotner), 231, 232, 236 (courtesy of Benjamin (Miedzyrzecki) Meed), 188 (courtesy of Bielski Family), 110 (courtesy of Debra Gierach), viii (courtesy of Dr. Rachel Kats), 146 (courtesy of Dr. Vera Lechtman), 352 (courtesy of Elizabeth Kaufmann Koenig), 51 (courtesy of Eric Zielenziger), 191 top (courtesy of Esther Klug), 256 (courtesy of Esther Vardi), 168, 169 (courtesy of Friedel Bohny-Reiter), 204 (courtesy of George Kadish/ Zvi Kadushin), 43 (courtesy of George Landecker), 152 (courtesy of Hanne Liebmann), 65 (courtesy of Hans Aussen), 104-105 (courtesy of Helena Mossel Bromet),

55, 57 (courtesy of Hilde Jacobsthal Goldberg), 220 (courtesy of Howard Kaplan), 191 bottom (courtesy of Instytut Pamieci Narodowej), 145, 149 (courtesy of Jack Lewin), 134 (courtesy of Jacques Leibman), 252 (courtesy of Jan Kostanski), 270 (courtesy of Jimmy Carter Library), 210-211 (courtesy of Julien Bryan Archive), 197, 198, 199 (courtesy of Larry Rosenbach), 8 (courtesy of Leo Goldberger), 4 (courtesy of Leonard Lauder), xviii (courtesy of Leopold Page Photographic Collection), 245 (courtesy of Louis Gonda), 180 (courtesy of Max Wischkin), 194-195 (courtesy of Moshe Kaganovich), i, 5, 9, 89, 174, 214, 218, 244, 247, 248, 258, 259, 269 (courtesy of National Archives and Records Administration, College Park), 267 (courtesy of Peretz Chorshati), 148 (courtesy of Peter Feigl), 154 (courtesy of Rescuers: Portraits of Moral Courage in the Holocaust), 141, 150 (courtesy of Richard Weilheimer), 73 (courtesy of Rita Serphos), 263, 264 (courtesy of Ron Leidelmeyer), 264 top (courtesy of Ruth Sherman), 159 bottom (courtesy of Sebastian Steiger), xv (courtesy of Shulamith Posner-Mansbach), 167 (courtesy of Simone Weil Lipman), 257 top, 257 bottom (courtesy of Society for the Research of the History of the Zionist Youth Movement in Hungary), 10 (courtesy of Stadtarchiv Stadthagen), 54, 86 (courtesy of Trudi Gidan), xiv (courtesy of Unknown Provenance), 158, 160 (courtesy of Vera Friedlaender),

159 top (courtesy of Walter Reed), xvi, xxiv (courtesy of William O. McWorkman), 182, 189, 200 (courtesy of Yehuda and Lola Bell Collection), 116 (United States Holocaust Memorial Museum Collection); Wisconsin Historical Society: 26; Yad Vashem Photo Archive, Jerusalem, 2631/7: 272.

INDEX

Note: Page numbers in *italics* refer to illustrations.

ACKNOWLEDGMENTS

This book wouldn't exist without the courage of survivors who have told their stories, and, in many cases, dedicated their lives to Holocaust education. Special thanks to Ruth Oppenheimer David, Paula Burger, and Wlodka Blit Robertson. Their courage, generosity of spirit, and commitment to social justice is an inspiration. I'm also grateful to David Moritz and his family for allowing me to quote from Alfred Moritz's beautifully illustrated memoir.

I'm grateful to Judy Margles, director of the Oregon Jewish Museum and Center for Holocaust Education (OJMCHE) for her careful reading of the manuscript and for enabling me to profile Oregonians such as the late Chella Velt Meekcoms Kryszek. Any errors of fact or interpretation are my own. Judy's colleagues, Anne LeVant Prahl, curator, and my friend and communications manager, Becca Biggs, have been amazingly supportive and patient with my requests. The Museum is a wonderful resource for Oregon.

We Must Not Forget is dedicated, with thanks, to my longtime agent, Steven Malk, and his family. It has been a delight to see Steven's career and family blossom since we first met more than twenty years ago.

This book would simply not be possible without the vision and insight of Lisa Sandell, my editor, who brings extraordinary compassion, dedication, and talent to her work—and to everything she does. I'm lucky to have Lisa as an editor and a friend. And I encourage readers with a love of nonfiction to look for other books under the Scholastic Focus imprint.

This book, as well as *We Had to Be Brave: Escaping the Nazis on the Kindertransport*, owes so much to archivist Michael Simonson of the Leo Baeck Institute in New York. Michael's generosity and perceptive comments have informed my research in innumerable ways. The memoirs and resources of the Leo Baeck Institute are truly amazing.

I also wish to thank Jacques Semelin, Professor Emeritus of History and Political Science at Sciences Po, CERI, SNRS, Paris, for his generosity and help with this project. And I'm appreciative of all the archivists, volunteers, and staff of museums and historical societies who dedicate countless hours to the work of raising awareness of history, and working to prevent intolerance, persecution, and genocide.

In addition to Paula Burger, Penny Nisson, Director of Education at the Mizel Museum, was immensely helpful in bringing Paula's memoir, *Paula's Window*, to the attention of a new audience. Thanks also to the hardworking and responsive staff at the United States Holocaust Memorial Museum, especially Robin Harp. Likewise, Paul Hedges, Digital Collections Coordinator, Library, Archives and Museum Collections at the Wisconsin Historical Society, was unfailingly supportive, as was Susan Harrod, Events and Outreach Manager, The Association of Jewish Refugees in the UK.

Thanks also to everyone on the Scholastic team who work so diligently to encourage reading and the exploration of history and literature. Thank you to Lori Benton, Ellie Berger, Erin Berger, Amy Chan, Lauren Donovan, Rachel Feld, Jael Fogle, Keirsten Geise, Emily Heddleson, Jordana Kulak, David Levithan, Matthew Poulter, Cian O'Day, Lizette Serrano, Emily Teresa, Danielle Yadao, Robin Hoffman, Laura Beets and the entire Book Fairs team, and many others—including, of course, "Mr. John Schu." This book owes much to many talented professionals in design, production, and photo research. And, of course, a huge thanks to copy editor Jessica White. Thank you!

Most days, I slog away at this old table in our dining room. Thanks to my friends and family who have gotten used to my being in another time and place. I'm writing your names in alphabetical order, which I hope will help me not forget anyone, but if I do, forgive me. Thanks to Maya Abels and Stewart Holmes; Deniz Conger; my sister Janice Fairbrother and nieces Kelly and Haley; my sister Bonnie Johnson and niece Jamie; my niece Ellie Thomas and her brilliant son, Nick; and many friends including Vicki Hemphill and Steve Johnston, along with Keelia, Meghan, and Aili and their amazing loved ones; Kristin Hill and Bill Carrick; C. Howard; Elisa Johnston, Fiona Kenshole, Jane Kurtz, Katie Morrison, Sheridan Mosher, Rosanne Parry, Judy Sierra and Bob Kaminski, Becky and Greg Smith, Vickie Tino, Teresa Vast and Michael Kieran, and, course, huge thanks to my across-the-country workmate, Deborah Wiles, and her wonderful husband, the incomparable Jim Pearce.

To Andy, Dimitri, Rebekah, Eric, and Oliver—I love you more than anything. Dearest Oliver, I hope you will always ask why.

ABOUT THE AUTHOR

Deborah Hopkinson is an award-winning author of picture books, middle grade fiction, and nonfiction. Her nonfiction titles include *We Had to Be Brave: Escaping the Nazis on the Kindertransport*; *Titanic: Voices from the Disaster*, a Sibert Medal Honor Book and YALSA Award for Excellence in Nonfiction finalist; *Courage & Defiance: Stories of Spies, Saboteurs, and Survivors in World War II Denmark*, a Sydney Taylor Notable Book, NCTE Orbis Pictus Recommended Book, and a winner of the Oregon Book Award and Oregon Spirit Award; *Dive! World War II Stories of Sailors & Submarines in the Pacific*, an NCTE Orbis Pictus Recommended Book and Oregon Spirit Award Honor Book; and *D-Day: The World War II Invasion That Changed History*.

Deborah lives with her family near Portland, Oregon, along with an assortment of pets that includes two canine office companions (Brooklyn and Rue); one cat (Beatrix); three chickens (Daisy, Chuckles, and Georgina); canaries named for #GOT characters; and an assortment of finches and fish. When she's not traveling the country to talk about history with students, Deborah is at the gym or attempting to create a garden. She also reads a lot. Visit her online at deborahhopkinson.com and follow her on Twitter at @Deborahopkinson and Instagram at @deborah_hopkinson.

A page of a sketchbook created by Elizabeth Kaufmann during her stay in Nazi-occupied France. The drawing of a street scene with four figures is entitled "Elizabeth and her mother arrested by French gendarmes."